War

A Beginner's Guide

T0056837

ONEWORLD BEGINNER'S GUIDES combine an original, inventive and engaging approach with expert analysis. Innovative and affordable, books in the series are perfect for anyone curious about the way the world works and the big ideas of our time.

aesthetics
africa
american politics
anarchism
ancient philosophy
animal behaviour
anthropology
anti-capitalism
aquinas
archaeology
art
artificial intelligence
the baha'i faith
the beat generation
the bible
biodiversity
bioterror & biowarfare
the brain
british politics
the Buddha
cancer
censorship
christianity
civil liberties
classical music
climate change
cloning
the cold war
conservation
crimes against humanity
criminal psychology
critical thinking
the crusades
daoism
democracy
descartes
dewey
dyslexia
economics

energy
engineering
the english civil wars
the enlightenment
epistemology
ethics
the european union
evolution
evolutionary psychology
existentialism
fair trade
feminism
forensic science
french literature
the french revolution
genetics
global terrorism
hinduism
history
the history of medicine
history of science
homer
humanism
huxley
international relations
iran
islamic philosophy
the islamic veil
journalism
judaism
lacan
life in the universe
literary theory
machiavelli
mafia & organized crime
magic
marx
medieval philosophy
the middle east

modern slavery
NATO
the new testament
nietzsche
nineteenth-century art
the northern ireland conflict
nutrition
oil
opera
the palestine–israeli conflict
parapsychology
particle physics
paul
philosophy
philosophy of mind
philosophy of religion
philosophy of science
planet earth
postmodernism
psychology
quantum physics
the qur'an
racism
rawls
reductionism
religion
renaissance art
the roman empire
the russian revolution
shakespeare
shi'i islam
the small arms trade
stalin
sufism
the torah
the united nations
the victorians
volcanoes
the world trade organization
world war II

War

A Beginner's Guide

Aaron Edwards

ONEWORLD

A Oneworld Paperback Original

Published in North America, Great Britain and Australia by
Oneworld Publications, 2017

ISBN 978-1-78074-894-8
eISBN 978-1-78074-895-5

Typeset by Silicon Chips

Printed and bound in Great Britain by Clays Ltd, St Ives plc

Oneworld Publications
10 Bloomsbury Street
London WC1B 3SR
England

Dedicated to my brother, Ryan Edwards,
who has seen the reality of war

and

To the memory of my great-grandfather,
LT/KX102452 Wartime Engineman Robert Edwards
RN, who was killed in action serving his King and
Country on 7 March 1942

Contents

Acknowledgements

Although research and writing can be solitary pursuits, the end product is rarely a single-handed effort. Several people contributed to the writing of this book. Chief amongst them was my good friend and colleague Tim Bean. Tim's helpful 'reading list' at the outset of this project augmented my own historiographical understanding of war, and his challenging and thorough comments on earlier drafts were the necessary spur I needed to complete the project. In a similar vein, Professor Christopher Duffy, Dr J. P. Harris, Dr Stephen Hart, Lieutenant Colonel (Ret'd) Peter McCutcheon MBE and Dr Stephen Walsh recommended a range of books and articles, which added immeasurably to the quality of the finished product. I could not have written this book without the support of Alan Ward, Sean McKnight and Dr David Brown, along with my other academic colleagues at Sandhurst, who supported my research sabbatical in 2013, thereby enabling me to get the book off to a good start. Alan and Sean also approved a two-day stopover at the Australian War Memorial in Canberra in April 2014, which gave me an invaluable insight into the ANZAC war experience.

The staff of the UK National Archives, Kew; the Liddell Hart Centre for Military Archives, King's College London; the Middle East Centre Archive at St Antony's College, Oxford; the Royal Ulster Rifles Museum, Belfast; and the Australian War Memorial Research Centre in Canberra were all particularly helpful. Research projects like this would not be possible without the unceasing help and support of Andrew Orgill and his team – John Pearce, Ken Franklin and Mel Bird – at the Royal Military

Academy Sandhurst Central Library. I would also particularly like to thank the former UK Chief of the General Staff, General Sir Roger Wheeler, whose insight into grand strategic matters in the post-Cold War era still resonates with me some years after I concluded my interviews with him.

I was fortunate to have the opportunity to test-drive some of my thoughts on regular war in front of a civilian and military audience at the '1944: seventy years on' conference at Sandhurst in April 2014. Likewise, the ideas contained in the 'Future war' chapter were aired at the highest strategic levels at the annual American, British, Canadian, Australian and New Zealand Armies Program Reserve Information Team Conference (ABCA) in Whitehall and I wish to convey my appreciation to those senior military officers who cross-examined my elucidation of the 'cognitive challenge of war' in October 2014.

Thanks also to Mike Harpley, Fiona Slater and Shadi Doost-dar at Oneworld for guiding the book through from concept to completion. Shadi, in particular, has been a great source of editorial ideas, as too were the readers who commented on both the proposal and an early draft of the manuscript.

Without the continuing support of my family – Jim, Barbara, Stephanie and Ryan Edwards – and my good friends – Tim Bean, Colonel (Ret'd) David Benest OBE, Stephen Bloomer, Professor Thomas Hennessey, Dr Paddy Hoey, Sean Brennan and Dr Martin McCleery – it would be impossible to work steadily and consistently on projects like this, especially during challenging personal and professional times. This book is dedicated to my great-grandfather, Wartime Engineman Robert Edwards RN, who, like countless other sailors, soldiers and airmen, was killed in action during the Second World War. It is also for my brother, Ryan Edwards, who, more than anyone else I know, has experienced the harsh reality of war first-hand with fortitude, good humour, and wisdom well beyond his years.

Introduction

On a visit to the Imperial War Museum in London shortly after Remembrance Sunday, I saw an exhibition of colourful illustrations by local schoolchildren entitled 'Postcards on war', which decorated the walls just beyond the first floor stairwell. It appeared that the children had been prompted by a member of staff to draw whatever came into their minds when they were asked the question: 'What is war?' Amidst the usual collection of artwork depicting artillery, tanks, planes, bomb shelters and rifles was a small note by one child who had foregone a pictorial description of war in favour of a written definition. 'War', it said, 'is when trust between people breaks down and they fight.'

I found this observation to be remarkably insightful. In one sentence the child had managed to convey a definition of war that echoes our age-old understanding of why war breaks out. To take but one example, it was His Holiness the Dalai Lama who wrote that, 'At best, building arms to maintain peace serves only as a temporary measure. As long as adversaries do not trust each other, any number of factors can upset the balance of power. Lasting peace can be secured only on the basis of genuine trust.' For the Dalai Lama, war remains an aberration; a terrible phenomenon to be extinguished from human relationships. Though even he at least acknowledges – as the child did in the Imperial War Museum – that the restoration of trust between warring factions is the surest way to usher in the promise of peace. Nonetheless, peace, as I aim to show in this book, amounts to little if the belligerents seek a more decisive resolution to their differences through bloodshed.

It is estimated that war, and the consequences of war, affects the lives of 1.5 billion people around the world. Fragile states, poor governance, gender-based violence, high levels of crime, conflict over identity, Internally Displaced Peoples (IDPs) and refugees are all symptomatic of the problems that war brings with it.[1] Although the mass slaughter of people on an industrial scale has not been seen since the Second World War, when 60–80 million people lost their lives, the number killed in armed conflict remains high and it is on the rise once again. According to the *World Development Report* published by the World Bank in 2011, the annual number of deaths from civil wars, including those in Angola, Bosnia, the Democratic Republic of the Congo (DRC) and Somalia, fell from more than 160,000 a year in the 1980s to less than 50,000 a year by the 2000s. Nevertheless, research by the International Institute for Strategic Studies (IISS) in London estimates that while the number of conflicts may be falling, the numbers of fatalities is rising. In 2008 there were sixty-three active armed conflicts, which incurred 56,000 fatalities, but by 2014 that number had trebled to 180,000 fatalities, even though the number of armed conflicts dropped to forty-two.[2] We have only to look at the numbers killed in two of the most high-profile wars of the post-9/11 world to see that war is still very much with us, and likely to remain with us for some time into the future. In Iraq, over a quarter of a million people have been killed since the US-led invasion in 2003 toppled Saddam Hussein. In Syria, a staggering half a million people are thought to have died as a result of protracted fighting since 2011.[3] Another worrying feature of the world we now live in is the exponential rise in the number of terrorism-related deaths. For instance, 18,000 people lost their lives in terrorist incidents in 2013, an increase of sixty-one percent from the previous year, with the Middle East and North Africa having become the epicentre of this kind of irregular war in the modern world.[4]

Behind the statistics, war has lost none of its power to shock and traumatize. The world we live in has been shaped for millennia by battles, campaigns and empire building, whether we wish to admit this or not. Protracted wars in Israel-Palestine, Iraq, the DRC, Yemen and Afghanistan are not new phenomena and, in some cases, appear (to historians at least) as reruns of earlier wars fought by individuals and groups over state legitimacy, power and status, or because of ethnic, political, tribal, clan, religious and ideological differences, amongst other reasons. To take the example of Afghanistan, it may be common in Western societies to see this war as having begun in 2001 and been terminated by the withdrawal of international combat forces in 2014; however, the reality is that – from an Afghan perspective – this is only the current phase in a civil war dating back to the late 1970s. Likewise, the character of war in Afghanistan has certainly changed over time, even if the grievances look distinctly familiar.

War, whatever we personally think about it, has been the principal means by which these differences have been resolved for thousands of years. The earliest recorded histories of war can be traced to the account of the Greco-Persian Wars by Herodotus, and even further back to the *Epic of Gilgamesh*, a poem of such power and tragedy that it ranks alongside the *Iliad* and *Odyssey* by Homer. The *Epic* itself dates back to ancient Mesopotamia (*c.* 2100 BCE). Sumerian readings place the hero at the centre of the narrative. Given that the story predates the rise and institutionalization of the modern state, the poem can be said to represent tensions straddling the recorded history of civilization, between individual and collective, ruler and ruled, man and king, and, ultimately, king and god. In the end, the *Epic of Gilgamesh* demonstrates how even a part-man, part-god, who desires the ultimate prize of immortality, comes to accept the inevitability of death. Importantly, what these ancient histories illustrate is that the root cause of war is man, a point brought out in the writings of Christian thinkers from St Augustine and Martin Luther to Jonathan Swift and Reinhold Niebuhr.

At its most basic level, war is something that individuals engage in collectively. War is a complex social process, if you will, which animates human beings into committing violent acts, ranging from killing and maiming, to inciting great fear, stress and hatred in their fellow man and woman. Whether we accept human nature as the root cause of war, or not, the manifestation of war has, of course, deeply human consequences that are often overlooked, including the degeneration of fighting into genocide and ethnic cleansing. Although historians remain divided over whether war is the direct consequence of rational acts or, indeed, the by-product of some kind of primordial urge to kill, this book takes the reader beyond these diametrically opposed viewpoints. It seeks to facilitate an informed discussion of war as a complex and multidimensional phenomenon that should be understood in its proper social, political and cultural context. At the same time, it is also important to think of war as being intimately connected to the international system in which it has evolved for centuries, and which often seems to provide a decisive way to resolve disputes that can, paradoxically, sometimes be prolonged by the resort to violence.

In recent years, the lines between regular and irregular warfare have become increasingly blurred. No longer are civilians guaranteed the protected status afforded to them by International Humanitarian Law (also known as the Law of War or the Law of Armed Conflict) and we have, in most cases, seen the exponential rise in targeted attacks against civilians. Inevitably, with so many more people drawn into armed conflict, the scars of war run deep and affect the physical and psychological well-being of individuals, tribes, communities, ethnic groups, religious sects, and even whole nations. In this respect, it matters just as much *how* wars are fought as *why* they are fought, in the main because of the effects this can have on the long-term reconstruction and reconciliation of war-torn societies, long after the guns fall silent.

In attempting to illustrate the complexity of war, this book avoids adopting a conventional approach. You will not find chapters on discrete aspects of land warfare, naval warfare or air warfare. Instead, examination of the spatial and temporal aspects of war are integrated into chapters that deal with war as a concept – chapters on 'strategies and tactics', 'regular war', 'irregular war' and 'future war' intermingle with chapters on 'what is war?', 'leaders and followers' and 'ending wars'. War is, therefore, analysed holistically, as the product of both theory and practice. But it would be remiss of a book on war to avoid the more unpleasant aspects, especially since these have left an indelible mark on mankind in one way or another. From the United States to Ireland, Norway, Bangladesh and beyond to the remote island of Tonga in the South Pacific, war has found its way into the lives of a great many people. War and the consequences of war haunt us like the wiry old ghost in Shakespeare's *Macbeth*. For those who have soldiered in service of their country, or who claim a familial lineage to ancestors on battlefields of yore, war is an ever-present leitmotif connecting individuals, families, tribes and other groups to their past. History, as this book seeks to demonstrate, is replete with episodes of war and peace that go some way to helping us understand the complexities of human nature.

These conflicting impulses must all be taken into account if we are to grasp the true meaning of war in our world. I invite the reader to journey with me into the dark heart of war to observe this multifaceted phenomenon at close quarters.

1
What is war?

'War', declared the Prussian general and military theorist Carl von Clausewitz in his masterful study *On War* (1832), is 'a continuation of political intercourse, carried on with other means.' This simple observation has been applauded by his supporters for its penetrating insight and derided by his critics as intoxicating, though it would be wrong to reduce the sum total of Clausewitz's masterpiece to this oft-quoted phrase without considering the other dimensions of war that he so convincingly wrote about in the immediate post-Napoleonic era. By itself, Clausewitz's famous aphorism does little to elucidate the complexity of the phenomenon it describes: namely, that war is the means by which the goal of attaining a political object can be reached. But war should never be considered in isolation from the ends to which it is directed, or the frequently bloody extent to which human beings will go in order to get what they want. Clausewitz, perhaps even more than his critics allow, recognized the diverse nature of war and was not beyond making it clear that he regarded the destruction of the enemy's forces as only really 'the means to an end'. To reduce war primarily to the death and destruction (i.e. the bloodshed) it unleashes, therefore, is to camouflage war as a true chameleon in the multitude of contexts in which it occurs.

For Clausewitz, war could be understood as a 'paradoxical Trinity', 'composed of primordial violence, hatred and enmity, which are to be regarded as a blind natural force; of the play of chance, and probability within which the creative spirit is free to roam; and of its element of subordination, as an instrument of policy, which makes it subject to reason alone'.[5] The rise of the modern state, the growth of nationalism (particularly in Europe), the onward march of the Enlightenment and, later, the Industrial Revolution, have all called into question this kind of war. Although Clausewitz's work is still regarded as a useful analytical framework for understanding war in the general sense, it has its limitations. It is worth considering some other important background factors regarding the origins of war and how Clausewitz arrived at this important definition.

Origins

For many people war is merely 'the absence of peace' (*absentia pax*), a view fashioned more by gut instinct than by an immersion in the recorded history of war over the past three millennia. Looking at it another way, we might also conclude that peace is, therefore, the absence of war (*absentia belli*), and that war is fought to rebalance the equilibrium in favour of 'peace'. Importantly, war is also shaped by politics, culture and society (i.e. the context in which war arises) and this inevitably extends into the peace which follows. Politics gives war its purpose, shapes its character, reinforces its utility, and sets the preconditions for its termination. As renowned journalist and writer George Orwell observed in the closing stages of the Second World War, 'At this moment, for instance, the world is at war and wants peace. Yet the world has no experience of peace, and never has had, unless the Noble Savage once existed.'[6] Orwell may have been writing during a period of 'total war' but his words have lost none of their purchase seventy years on, as the world once again reverberates to the sound of gunfire and explosions in wars of an altogether more 'limited' kind.

It was the Chichele Professor of the History of War at Oxford University and veteran of the Battle of the Somme (1916), Cyril Falls, who ventured forward with the truism that 'the dispute between two handfuls of cave-dwellers for the possession of shelter leads to grim work with stone axes.'[7] That war began in prehistoric times can safely be assumed, though the very word itself conjures up images of Persian, Greek and Roman armies battling for self-interest, survival and territorial expansion. In understanding the origins of war, it is necessary always to keep in mind the Roman policy as espoused by Vegetius, '*Sic vis pacem, para bellum*' ('If you want peace, prepare for war'), which necessitates analysing the history of warfare according to the cultures that produced and sustained it. It is not known when warfare became part of the process of human interaction, though it has been said that violence has its roots in the evolutionary process that saw mankind evolve from the same ancestors as chimpanzees some six million years ago.[8] We do know, however, that the world was much more violent in past times than it is today. The current rate for death by violence in the world population is around 0.7 percent, contrasted with 1–2 percent in the twentieth century, 2–5 percent in ancient empires, 5–10 percent in Eurasia in the age of Steppe migrations and a startling 10–20 percent in the Stone Age.[9]

Historians have traced organized warfare back to the deserts of Mesopotamia in the fourth millennium BCE, when the Sumerians made an appearance between the banks of the Tigris and the Euphrates. Building up their military establishment as a means of protecting and enforcing their civilizing impulse, they oversaw the building of fortified towns, guarded by charioteers and infantry. At that time they operated in phalanxes – solid rectangular formations of men armed with spears and shields. Similarly, the barbarians who finally assaulted the Roman Empire were taught the arts of military organization by the very civilization they sought to overthrow. Barbarians took service in the Roman army, learned about military affairs, and then returned home to put their knowledge to use among their own people. Warfare also has origins in other parts of the world, having been traced to ancient civilizations in Egypt, India and China. In ancient China, around the time that Sun Tzu (*c.* 400–320 BCE) wrote his magisterial *The Art of War*, the basis upon which the known world was hitherto organized began to crumble. Men of talent were now taking to the battlefield and vast armies were being raised around a core of trained professionals. For Sun Tzu, war became 'a matter of vital importance to the State; the province of life or death; the road to survival or ruin', in which 'Victory is the main object in war.'[10]

CARL VON CLAUSEWITZ (1780–1831)

Born on 1 June 1780 in Burg, near Magdeburg, Carl von Clausewitz was a Prussian soldier and philosopher of war. The son of an army officer who had fought in the Seven Years' War (1756–63) and the grandson of a theology professor at Halle, he had enlisted into the 34th Prussian Infantry Regiment in 1792 at the age of eleven and later saw action in the Napoleonic campaign of 1812. Clausewitz was greatly influenced by the Hanoverian general officer Gerhard Scharnhorst, a transferee to the Prussian army who set up the war school in Berlin. In 1816 he began to write *On War*, which would later become one of the most significant contributions to the study of war to appear in print. Clausewitz was still making revisions to his book in 1830, the year he went off to a war from which he would never return. *On War* was published posthumously by Clausewitz's widow, Maria, in 1832.

By the turn of the nineteenth century war had become a more formal process of interaction between nation states, in which competing interests were usually resolved by bloodshed. In this sense war was 'a continuation of political intercourse, carried on with other means'. Many commentators misleadingly understand this to mean that at some point there is a departure from 'peaceful' politics towards 'aggressive' war. War rarely proceeds in this kind of linear sequence, wherein political intercourse, having been exhausted, simply runs its course and war takes over. In the sense that it is employed here, in the sense that Clausewitz himself understood it, war is understood as a dialectical process in which policy and war continuously interact and where the former determines the character of the latter.

Why men (and women) fight wars

For many years it was believed that the First World War (1914–18) had been fought willingly by citizens and subjects across Europe who exhibited a hysterical clamouring for war. Yet we now know that this euphoric sentiment was not shared by everyone, including the statesmen and generals who were to preside over it. So, if militarism was not the dominant force in European politics at this time, what made men fight in this war? There is no single explanation for this, but patriotism, peer pressure, conscription and coercion all played their part. All armies in the First World War used coercion to stave off the prospect of desertion in the face of enemy fire. For instance, in the First World War, the British Army sentenced some 3,080 soldiers to death for desertion, cowardice, mutiny and other associated offences, with 346 meeting their end at the hands of a firing squad.[11] In the Second World War, the Soviet army shot over 10,000 men who had beaten a retreat from enemy positions. Elsewhere in the same war, in the Pacific theatre, Japanese soldiers who were defeated in battle preferred to take their own lives in ritual suicide, by charging into oncoming enemy fire, rather than face the humiliation of surrender. So, in war, we find a degree of coercion is necessary in order to get people to fight – a point that could suggest violence and aggression are not natural or preferred human states.

In Joseph Heller's novel *Catch-22*, about a bomber squadron based in Italy, the main protagonist, Yossarian, grows tired and disaffected by the constant combat missions he is expected to fly over enemy territory. Throughout the book he makes his disgruntlement obvious to his fellow airmen and, ultimately, to his commanding officer. At this stage he decides to leave his unit but he is unable to do so because of 'Catch-22'. The catch is that even though our protagonist is informed that he can go home from war after flying forty missions, military regulations still say that he has to obey every order from a superior officer. Failure to do so would make him guilty of disobeying a lawful order. The state, we can infer from Heller's book, has reserved for itself the last say in compelling men (and, occasionally, women) to go to war. Military historian Sir John Keegan has captured this point well:

> Coercion is a word to which the vocabulary of democracy gives grudging house room. The liberal state likes to believe it works by consent and persuasion, that compulsion is a method of dealing with citizens to which only the lower forms of polity have to resort. The truth, of course, is that all armies, whether of democracies or dictatorships, depend on the coercive principle (most armies have a code of law and punishment separate from that administered by the civil courts), that it is a vital element in making battles work, and that it is one which the character of modern warfare invests with more not less force.[12]

When we look back through history at the reason given for why people fight, it becomes clear just how important the state has been in facilitating this process.

THE POLICY OF PERICLES, 430 BCE

In his *History of the Peloponnesian War* Thucydides recalls a speech delivered by the Athenian general Pericles in which he tried to steady the individual concerns of the Athenian people:

> My own opinion is that when the whole state is on the right course it is a better thing for each separate individual than when private interests are satisfied but the state as a whole is going downhill. However well off a man may be in his private life, he will still be involved in the general ruin if his country is destroyed; whereas, so long as the state itself is secure, individuals have a much greater chance of recovering from their private misfortunes. Therefore, since a state can support individuals in their suffering, but no one person by himself can bear the load that rests upon the state, is it not right for us all to rally to her defence? Is it not wrong to act as you are doing now? For you have been so dismayed by disaster in your homes that you are losing your grip on the common safety; you are attacking me for having spoken in favour of war and yourselves for having voted for it.[13]

Quite apart from state attempts to coerce or stimulate patriotism in its citizens, when it comes down to it, men and women in battle will also do what they need to for the sake of their comrades, knowing that they, in turn, will do the same for them. Legal scholars concur with this analysis. In the words of Professor Mark J. Osiel, 'Efficacy in combat now depends more on tactical imagination and loyalty to combat buddies than on immediate, unreflective adherence to the letter of superiors' orders, backed by discipline of formal punishment.'[14] Ultimately, the glue that binds men and women together in battle is morale, which is engendered in the natural will to fight, a process that becomes more potent whenever individuals judge their own interests – more so than those of the state – to be at stake. Ian Gardiner, a British Royal Marines officer who fought in the Falklands War of 1982, explained morale in the following way: 'You don't need Napoleon or Montgomery to tell you that if your men won't fight, you will lose', he said. 'The British had the stomach for a fight because they were well trained and well led. The Argentines didn't, because they weren't.'[15]

War and the human condition

'War is hell' is a frequent refrain that has become synonymous with our perceptions of war since the mass industrialized slaughter of the First World War. Paradoxically, some of the most powerful poetry, prose and films have emerged out of wartime. As one delegate who attended the Chicago Peace Congress in 1894 declared, 'an honest man must feel that war, even when inevitable, is always sad and miserable.' While this delegate felt war caused a 'profound disturbance and derangement of social and moral order', history is nonetheless replete with 'a dazzling halo of poetry and of glory; the most renowned poems in all ancient and modern literatures are hymns to war; the most stately monuments glorify warriors.'[16]

The war poet Wilfred Owen knew all about the fatalism war induced in those who fought it. He had soldiered on the Western Front in the First World War as an officer in the Second Manchesters, an infantry regiment, which placed him on the front line of the largest war yet experienced by continental Europe. In 'Anthem for Doomed Youth', a poem Owen wrote in 1917, he captures the suffering and carnage of that war, and observes the grim reality of the trenches where death haunted him and his men, cutting many of them down in the prime of their lives:

> What passing-bells for these who die as cattle?
> Only the monstrous anger of the guns.
> Only the stuttering rifles' rapid rattle
> Can patter out their hasty orisons.

No mockeries now for them; no prayers nor bells,

> Nor any voice of mourning save the choirs, -
> The shrill, demented choirs of wailing shells;
> And bugles calling for them from sad shires.

Owen's poetry brought together the ingredients of loss, death and the sheer horror of war. Despondency, fear and the intoxicating effects of poison gas were a common thread in his poems.

This preoccupation with death haunts other First World War poetry too. Rupert Brooke captured the intimacy of man's close bond with his own mortality in war:

> Nothing to shake the laughing heart's long peace there
> But only agony, and that has ending;
> And the worst friend and enemy is but Death.[17]

In his classic *Men Against Fire*, Brigadier General S. L. A. Marshall found that for every 100 men in combat, only fifteen to twenty of them fired their weapons in a firefight.[18] Why is this the case? Leading military scientist Lieutenant Colonel Dave Grossman suggested that men are unlikely to kill, even when faced with the risk of losing 'all that he holds dear', for the following reason: 'Looking another human being in the eye, making an independent decision to kill him, and watching as he dies due to your action combine to form the single most basic, important, primal, and potentially traumatic occurrence of war. If we understand this, then we understand the magnitude of the horror of killing in combat.'[19]

One does not have to look far to find evidence of the effects of other wars on ordinary people. Ernest Hemingway's character Lieutenant Berrendo in his Spanish Civil War epic *For Whom the Bell Tolls* resigns himself to the observation *Qué cosa más mala es la Guerra* ('What a bad thing war is'). Hemingway depicts fighting as both a philosophical experience and a highly political act.[20] It is as if man is an innocent bystander in a world where war is imposed upon him, a naive view, as Hemingway himself recognized, particularly since he was greatly influenced by Clausewitz's view that war was, above all, a human activity.[21] The idea that man might become war's master has its origins in the rise of the international state system and organized warfare. In *Henry IV, Part 1,* William Shakespeare's protagonist declares that 'The edge of war, like an ill-sheathed knife, no more shall cut his master', as if men are somehow able to fully control war rather than simply having to suffer its unfolding bloody drama. In attempting to master war, men and women have also had to accept Leon Trotsky's aphorism that, even though 'war rests on many sciences ... war itself is not a science – it is a practical art, a skill.'[22]

The British Army's pre-eminent philosopher of war, Major General J. F. C. Fuller, suggested that soldiers 'stumbled into the war like a man over a precipice on a dark night. To them war meant killing, and consequently, hunting in England was considered the highest form of military training.'[23] The harsh reality for those involved in fighting wars is that they might well be called upon to kill and, in some cases, die in the course of engaging with those they believe to be their enemy. Renowned war reporter Martha Gelhorn returned some of the most powerful dispatches of the Second World War. In her reportage, death in war became an everyday occurrence:

Close to a big filling station a bus lay on its side, already burned out, and beside it in the street was the first dead man I saw in this war. On my first morning in Madrid, three winters ago, I saw a man like this one. Now as then there was no identification left except the shoes, since the head and the arms had been destroyed. In Spain the small, dark, deformed bundle wore the rope-soled shoes of the poor, and here the used leather soles were carefully patched. Otherwise the two remnants of bodies were tragically the same. I thought it would be fine if the ones who order the bombing and the ones who do the bombing would walk on the ground some time and see what it is like.[24]

Even those engaged in fighting tend to downplay the extraordinary circumstances in which they find themselves. One British Army bomb disposal operator stationed in the Shatt al-Arab Hotel in Basra city, Iraq, in the summer of 2006 recalled the effects of being under fire:

The Shatt, as it was known, could only be described as the Alamo. Our team were on QRF [Quick Reaction Force] and called to go into the city to deal with an unexploded rocket fired by insurgents in nearby flats a few hundred metres from the hotel ... We would have to turn up in the dead of night and set about digging down to the rocket, lining it with explosives and making it safe. Typical of this sort of work, you never thought of it as being dangerous, only that some twat had decided to fire it on a Friday night and you weren't getting any sleep! How inconvenient! An hour or two into the task we changed round to allow us to get a half hour kip in the back of one of the snatch Land Rovers. Lying on top of some ammo tins with my legs hanging out the back door, I heard the unmistakable screech of incoming rockets. Present day IDF [Indirect Fire] drills told us to hit the dirt straight away; however, things were a wee bit more 'cowboy' back in 2006. We grabbed our body armour, helmets and rifles and ran 'hard target' down a small street within the hotel compound. I looked up and about 15 metres above my head I saw the vapour trail (like a normal household firework flying into the air) followed by an almighty

explosion about 50 metres away – apparently the hotel
swimming pool got the good news! Again, I wouldn't say
this was a frightening experience – more like a 'fuck me
that was close.' You then got up off the deck and carried
on running. Once under 'hard cover' in the hotel lobby
we burst into fits of laughter ... [possibly as a reaction to]
our close call that night ... [It was] probably the closest
I'd ever come to getting hit that tour. Around 10 rockets
had been fired by the insurgents [in that one incident].[25]

The idea that war is boredom occasionally punctuated by excitement is borne out in perhaps one of the greatest anti-war novels
of the twentieth century. In George Orwell's *Homage to Catalonia*,
Orwell writes with the authority of having personally shouldered
a rifle and felt the weight of a pack in the Spanish Civil War
(1936–9), fighting on the side of the republicans in their war
with Franco's fascists. In his caustic denunciation of the fighting,
Orwell writes:

Meanwhile nothing happened, nothing ever happened.
The English had got into the habit of saying that this
wasn't a war, it was a bloody pantomime. We were hardly
under direct fire from the Fascists. The only danger was
from stray bullets, which, as the lines curved forward on
either side, came from several directions. All the casualties
at this time were from strays.[26]

In many ways this reflects the hypothesis advanced by sociolo-
gist Randall Collins, who informs us that human beings are not
well disposed to committing acts of violence, for it is a hard, not
an easy, activity. Though organized armed forces tend to invest
heavily in training their soldiers in the proficiency of warfare and
emphasize the 'professionalism' of killing, it is not at all clear how
effective soldiers actually are once engaged in battle. As Collins

observes, 'Soldiers and police hit their targets in actual combat much less frequently than in practice on firing ranges; missing one's targets is extremely common in violence by criminals (where we can calculate this from numbers of bullets fired); similar patterns appear from blows thrown in fights.'[27]

In much the same way that Hannah Arendt de-conflicted the concepts of power and violence, which she argued were better thought of as distinct but linked phenomena,[28] the correlation between war and violence is not as predetermined as we might think. Randall Collins likens individuals who engage in violence to repeat-offending criminals, who must learn and adapt to their illicit business or risk failure and imprisonment. In analysing the actions of individuals who find themselves in a scenario in which the prospect of violence has become conscionable, a mixture of anxiety and fear drives them on to commit gross acts of barbarity that would not have otherwise crossed their minds.

'Fear is the common bond between fighting men', observed military historian Richard Holmes. 'Only a tiny percentage of soldiers never know fear at all.'[29] The fear of being killed in battle pervades the minds of most soldiers involved in frontline combat. It heightens their senses, with many recording how their senses of smell, hearing and sight were acutely affected by battle. It can also lead to extreme nervousness, hypertension and even uncontrollable bowel movements and vomiting. In the 1998 Hollywood movie *Saving Private Ryan*, recognized by film critics and veterans of the Normandy campaign to be one of the most realistic portrayals of war ever to have made it onto the silver screen, the first twenty minutes feature all of the recurring physical and psychological effects of battle. Often, those wounded in battle are less affected by the trauma of the injuries they sustained than by what has come to be known as 'combat stress'.

Stress in battle is perhaps best captured in one of the most quintessential works of fiction on the subject of war to have emerged from the twentieth century. In Erich Remarque's *All Quiet on the Western Front*, the main protagonist in the novel is an unknown soldier, with a family, hopes and dreams, with concern for his own self-preservation, who finds himself caught up in a bombardment in the trenches. The young conscript remains paralysed by a mini-tsunami of emotions ranging from fear to shame. After a short time pinned to the ground absorbing the sights, sounds and smells of war, he tells himself that he must get up for 'it's to do with your mates, not some stupid order.'[30]

It is important for us to examine the conflicting emotions – or 'fighting a crazy, confused battle' as Remarque's protagonist puts it – that animate those individuals who play such a central role in war. Randall Collins takes us through the different ways in which a surge of emotion propels an individual to harm his opponent. Perhaps the most convincing is the idea of a 'forward panic', known prior to the twentieth century as 'Flight to the Front'. The composite mood of a forward panic comes from the transformation of tension/fear into an aggressive frenzy, usually centred on rage. The release of that urge may be primordial, in the sense that those in danger have arrived at this point after a degree of training, and are now fired up by adrenalin as they prepare to kill another human being. However, as we saw in relation to the work of Marshall and Grossman, when faced with the prospect of taking the life of another person, man is rarely willing to do so.

Morality and law in war

In early February 1942, 55,000 Japanese troops poured ashore on the coast of Malaya in one of the most stunning invasions in military history, all the more incredible because they were outnumbered by approximately four to one. Overwhelming the Allied soldiers, sailors and airmen who defended the island, they appeared unstoppable as they crushed their opposition in little more than a few days, forcing the British general commanding the Allied troops to surrender. In a now infamous incident at the Alexandra Military Hospital in Singapore on 14 February 1942, Japanese soldiers unleashed a wave of summary executions on medical staff and their patients. As one eyewitness later wrote:

> The Japs then motioned the staff to move along the corridor, which they did, then for no apparent reason set about them with bayonets. Lt. Rogers RAMC was bayoneted twice through the back of the thorax and died at once. Capt. Parkinson was bayoneted to death, also Capt. McEwan and Pte. Lewis. A patient on the operating table was also bayoneted to death; this man was later identified as Cpl. Holden, 2nd Loyals. Capt. Smiley was bayoneted but struck the blade aside and it hit his cigarette case which was in his left breast pocket.[31]

Amidst the thuds and explosions of falling artillery shells, the troops were said to be quite 'excitable and jumpy' that day as they marauded through the hospital. The official war diary of the medical unit records how they took patients outside and held over 200 of them as prisoners in appalling conditions in a small outbuilding, where some later died of their wounds. Japanese soldiers then bayoneted others who had been taken away and crammed still more prisoners into large sewage drains where they were kept without food or water. Interestingly, while some of the troops descended to barbarism, the Japanese general visiting the hospital three days later expressed his regret at what happened and said the non-combatants had nothing further to fear from his troops. Atrocities like these nonetheless continued until the end of the war.

What made these troops commit such awful acts? There is evidence of both Japanese and Allied troops going on to kill their enemies after they had sufficiently dehumanized them. American liberal commentator Gore Vidal served in the US Army during the war and saw similar atrocities in the South Pacific against the Japanese. He recalls how:

> Although we were not enthusiastic warriors, there was a true hatred of the enemy. We were convinced that the 'Japs' were subhuman; and our atrocities against them pretty much matched theirs against us. I was in the Pacific Theatre of Operations, where the war was not only imperial but racial: the white race was fighting the yellow race, and the crown would go to us as we were the earth's supreme race, or so we had been taught. One of the ugliest aspects of that war was the racial stereotyping on both sides. In Europe we were respectful – even fearful – of the Germans. Since blacks and women were pretty much segregated in our military forces, World War II was, for us, literally, the white man's burden.[32]

We know from the research undertaken by scholars working on genocide that individuals do not have to be coerced into carrying out murderous acts, nor do they do it simply out of obedience. It is more likely that they will commit atrocities given the right amount of motivation and how they adapt individually and ideologically to the cultural context in which they find themselves.[33] What also makes killing possible, of course, is the close proximity of individuals to the actual fighting. Despite the representation of war in films and books, the reality is that only a small number of soldiers ever see combat. In the Second World War there was an average of eight support soldiers for every one combat soldier; the Japanese, on the other hand, claimed a much higher ratio of one to one.[34]

There have been attempts by the international community to reduce the number of non-combatants killed in war. The Laws of War (or International Humanitarian Law as it is also known) have their origins in the Lieber Code of 1863. But it was the work of an enterprising Frenchman, Henri Dunant, horrified by the treatment meted out to survivors of the bloody Battle of Solferino (24 June 1859), that triggered a major shift towards more humane treatment of the wounded and sick. The establishment of the International Committee of the Red Cross (ICRC) in Geneva in the late nineteenth century, under Dunant's supervision, sought to alleviate the calamities of war, though it also resurrected the idea of states adopting laws that would safeguard the rights of the dead and wounded on the battlefield, as well as those captured in war. Despite the formulation and acceptance into customary international law of the Geneva Conventions (1949), which were aimed at preventing atrocities like those witnessed in the Second World War, the world continues to be plagued by barbarism.

US involvement in Vietnam in the 1960s demonstrated that atrocities were still possible after 1945. The intentional murder of 500 Vietnamese men, women and children at My Lai on 16 March 1968 is one of the most infamous massacres of the twentieth century, not only because of how it was carried out but also how it was subsequently covered up. The events of that day are easily explained. Troops from Charlie Company, Task Force Barker, infiltrated the area in Huey gunships while artillery rounds from nearby fire bases bombarded the vicinity of the village, sending the villagers scrambling for cover. The troops were anticipating a battle with locally based Viet Cong irregulars, but they had long since evaporated into the surrounding countryside. 1st Platoon, led by Lieutenant William L. Calley, Jr, entered the villages with guns blazing. His men fired indiscriminately into villagers' homes, tossed grenades into bunkers, and shot at those Vietnamese civilians fleeing the hamlet. They gathered large groups of villagers, herded them into ditches, and shot them in cold blood. In the space of a few hours, the soldiers had killed hundreds of men, women and children.[35] Lieutenant Calley was subsequently arrested and put on trial after a full investigation was ordered into My Lai.

During a cross-examination at his court martial, Lieutenant Calley claimed he was only following orders given to him by a superior commander:

> Like I said, sir, I gave the order to take those people through the ditch and had also told Meadlo if he couldn't move them to 'waste them' and I directly – other than that – it was only one incident. I never stood up there for any period of time. My main mission was to get my men on the other side of that ditch and get in that defensive position and that's what I did, sir.[36]

In many of the transcripts detailing the killing of Vietnamese civilians, there is a clear lack of empathy on the part of the killers. The soldiers lucidly explain away the unchecked slaughter of men, women and children with a cold calculation that is riddled with allusions to the commonly used military jargon of 'neutralizing the village'. In contrast to My Lai, restraint was more frequently practised by other American soldiers when faced with mortal danger. In his harrowing account of his tour in Vietnam, Frederick Downs faced life or death situations on a daily basis as a platoon leader. In one incident, where two young Vietnamese boys charged his troops, he reluctantly gave the order to open fire. 'An irrevocable wave of death swept in front of us', he recalled.

> After the initial burst of gunfire, I yelled, 'Cease fire.' Two women survived long enough to cross the bridge and enter one of the hootches [villagers' huts]. Three of my men crossed over the bridge and threw grenades in the hootches. We hurriedly looked over the bodies on the trail since they were lying in the open and we had no desire to be caught exposed. The men reported that some

of the dead had been carrying hand grenades and ammo in their packs. I felt somewhat relieved. Those supplies could not have been for anyone but the Cong.[37]

In his Amnesty International lecture delivered at Oxford University in 1994, historian Eric Hobsbawm remarked how 'Total war and cold war have brainwashed us into accepting barbarity.' He decried the crumbling away of the state in Eastern Europe that lay at the centre of the ethnic and nationalist conflicts now riddling the former Yugoslavia. Rather than saving his criticism for non-democratic regimes or rebels and revolutionaries as being sufficiently well practised in the excesses of war, he raised the perfectly legitimate point that democracies required 'demonized enemies' and that the Cold War served to facilitate barbarism.[38]

The industrialized scale of killing during the Second World War had profound repercussions for the postwar settlement after the surrender of Germany and Japan. Mass atrocities by the Japanese in South-East Asia and the Nazi turn to genocide in Eastern Europe weighed heavily on the minds of the architects of the United Nations (UN) in 1945. The UN Charter recognized the mass industrial slaughter and the negative impact it had had, not only on states but also on peoples. The idealists who met in San Francisco were determined to prevent a return to world war. War Crimes Tribunals were convened to seek justice and retribution for the peoples and states that had suffered from massive destruction and genocide, as statesmen sought to put in place mechanisms for managing international relations in a way that minimized the scope for threats, aggression and bloodshed. Despite the horrors of the Second World War, there has been no diminution in the belief that organized violence offers one way of pursuing a definitive resolution to a political problem.

JUST WAR THEORY

The Just War tradition emerged from the teachings of Christian moral philosophers who placed great stock in controlling and limiting war while keeping in mind the humanity of those who engaged in fighting. Although not exclusively Christian in its application (both Islam and Judaism provide guidance on the ethics of war fighting), Just War remains 'a systematic reminder of moral questions which we ought to think about when we consider embarking upon armed conflict or when we engage in it'.[39] There are two key aspects of Just War that are common to our understanding of war as a means to an end. The first is *jus ad bellum* (i.e. going to war), and works from the assumption that killing and injuring human beings is wrong and must only be undertaken under certain circumstances. The provisions for engaging in Just War are known as *just cause, proportionate cause, right intention, right authority, reasonable prospect of success* and *last resort*. These are essential criteria that must be considered before states broach the prospect of war with other states, and shape how the UN views war. The second aspect of the Just War tradition is *jus in bello* (i.e. waging war) and includes the principles of *discrimination*, meaning that belligerents must distinguish between combatants and non-combatants; *proportionality*, which means only applying that degree of force that is absolutely necessary to defeating their enemy; *humanity*, which emphasizes only using those means and methods of warfare required to defeat your opponent; and *military necessity*, which means only attacking a target in order to achieve the overriding mission. Collectively these two aspects of the Just War tradition still exert considerable influence over how Western states, in particular, approach war in the twenty-first century.

Even though we may be careful in our assessment of the processes that give rise to this kind of behaviour in wartime conditions, cruelty remains a perennial feature of war. States and international organizations have made considerable advances over the past century in trying to ensure that warring factions comply with the ICRC and 'alleviate the calamities of war', but killing and abuses continue. In cases of mass atrocity committed under wartime conditions, legal scholars maintain that they 'could not transpire without the organized cooperation of many', including 'both soldiers of various rank and sympathetic civilians'.[40] In one of the most infamous examples of mass atrocity perpetrated principally by state-based armies and militias during civil war, we can see how the dehumanization of the enemy became a prerequisite for killing large numbers of people in a relatively short space of time. In Rwanda in 1994 an attack on the plane carrying President Juvénal Habyarimana of Rwanda and President Cyprien Ntaryamira of Burundi sparked one of the greatest murder sprees of the twentieth century, when the majority Hutu ethnic group went on a revenge rampage against the minority Tutsis. Almost one million people died – men, women and children – in the space of a few weeks.

The scenes greeting the international community were relayed by one Canadian peacekeeper, the force commander of the UN mission to Rwanda, Lieutenant General Roméo Dallaire:

> If you looked, you could see the evidence, even in the whitened skeletons. The legs bent and apart. A broken bottle, a rough branch, even a knife between them. Where the bodies were fresh, we saw what must have been semen pooled on and near the dead women and girls. There was always a lot of blood. Some male corpses had their genitals cut off, but many women and young girls had their breasts chopped off and their genitals crudely cut apart. They died in a position of total vulnerability, flat on their backs, with their legs bent and knees wide apart. It was the expressions on their dead faces that assaulted me the most, a frieze of shock, pain and humiliation. For many years after I came home, I banished the memories of those faces from my mind, but they have come back, all too clearly.[41]

Sexual violence has been employed as a weapon of war for centuries, but war rape became a common feature of civil wars

in Africa and the Balkans in the twentieth century, as states failed
and relinquished their obligations to protect their populations.
The UN estimates that as many as 100,000–250,000 women and
girls were raped in the Rwandan genocide alone, with unprece-
dented levels of sexual violence. Prompted by this, on 31 December 2000 the UN passed Security Council Resolution 1325
on 'Women, Peace and Security', which reaffirms the key role
played by women in the prevention and resolution of conflicts,
in decision making, in negotiations and in other measures aimed
at building peace.[42]

As already mentioned, wartime conditions can make combatants actively dehumanize their enemies, thereby creating a kind
of tunnel vision in those who resort to brutality. An eyewitness
account of the abuse meted out by a small number of British
soldiers at a military base in Iraq in 2003 confirms how this can
so easily happen:

> He was moving about the room and occasionally giving
> the detainees a punch to their lower back area ... When
> Cpl Payne punched the detainees they all cried out in
> pain and some of them dropped to their knees. He was
> bringing his whole arm back and putting some weight
> behind the punches. I cannot recall which arm he used. I
> knew what was happening was wrong but felt I couldn't
> do or say anything. Some of the multiple [a unit smaller
> than a platoon of 30 soldiers] including myself did actually
> slap the detainees on the face as this was apparently an
> insult to Iraqis.[43]

When explaining their reasoning for abusing Iraqi detainees in
this case, the soldiers excused away their actions as being a direct
product of structural factors that made them do what they did.
However, one legal scholar examining the case drew an important

conclusion that detainee abuse was not inevitable and, with the right training, could have been prevented.[44]

The Sri Lankan civil war that raged between the early 1980s and 2009 typified the turn to annihilation as a workable policy of a government in effecting the termination of an irregular challenge to its authority. Undoubtedly this led to the deaths of tens of thousands of Tamils, an ethnic minority concentrated in the northern tip of the Jaffna Peninsula. Most civilians killed during the final phase of Sri Lankan military operations probably died from artillery fire. Accountability under International Law has, in theory, increased since the end of the Cold War. Gone are the days when mass slaughter or carpet-bombing can be concealed by the blanket denial of the perpetrators. But images of war retain the power to shock the world, as we saw in the Sri Lankan case of dead and wounded Tamil fighters being abused by soldiers. A report published by the UN in September 2015 found that there were 'long-standing and deep-rooted violations and abuses of human rights and international humanitarian law, some of which may amount to international crimes'.[45] War is always ugly, but never has this fact been more evident to the rest of the world than since the turn of the twenty-first century, when images of dead and dying civilians caught up in conflict are broadcast globally in real time.

The type of atrocities witnessed in Sri Lanka included attacks on hospitals and non-combatants. While these were both illegal and demonstrative of the lengths to which armies could go in order to defeat their opponents, they were by no means isolated incidents. After the invasion of Iraq by a US-led coalition in 2003 and the ensuing insurgency that sprang up against the continued occupation by Western troops, the withdrawal by US troops in 2011 signalled new possibilities for this tumultuous Middle Eastern state. The political benefits of the US withdrawal to Nouri al-Maliki's Iraqi government would prove short-lived and in the opening months of 2014 a new terrorist group called Daesh (an Arabic acronym for al-Dawla al-Islamiya fil Iraq wa al-Sham, also known as Islamic State (IS) and Islamic State in Iraq and Al-Sham (ISIS)) achieved considerable military successes against Iraqi security forces. Daesh had utilized a clever blend of insurgent and terrorist tactics to inflict massive defeats on their enemies, many of whom were captured with hardly a shot being fired by their bold and fanatical enemy. However, it was their Faustian pact with the former leaders of Saddam Hussein's ruling Ba'ath Party that gave Daesh's military operations considerable traction. Capitalizing on the surprise and confusion generated by this 'blitzkrieg' (a military operation that used speed and aggression to break the cohesion of the Iraqi security forces), Daesh began to launch further assaults on Iraqi cities from its base in Raqqa in Syria. In a matter of weeks it had ridden roughshod over International Humanitarian Law by executing thousands of prisoners and capturing and enslaving many thousands more.

Daesh is now considered to have been successful because it learned lessons from the defeat of its previous incarnation, al-Qaeda in Iraq (AQI), which drew together jihadis from a diverse range of backgrounds in opposition to the US-led occupation of Iraq. By decentralizing its command structure, Daesh demonstrated that Western forces organized along conventional lines could not hope to defeat a loose association of terrorists and insurgents who combined speed, aggression and intimate knowledge of the human and physical terrain. As Andrew Hosken would later remark in relation to Daesh victories in the first half of 2014, this was the return of 'an old menace that had refused to die', which transformed its military strategy to capitalize on the shock and surprise that the 'swarming nature of their invasion' was now demonstrating.[46]

This opening chapter has made the case that war is a human activity that is seen as a means of resolving disputes through the use of force. In this sense, wars are often fought to rebalance the equilibrium in favour of some idea of 'peace', though they rarely, if ever, end disputes, conflict or confrontation, and they may even prolong them long into the future. It is with that in mind that we see how the highly political concepts of war and peace are continually shaped by an uneven distribution of power between competing groups. While there have been attempts to place legal constraints on war, the very fact that human beings are involved in the process means that treaty law will always find itself up against the morals and ethics of the men and women that states call upon to fight and die for their country.

2
Strategy and tactics in war

'The task of the science of strategy', wrote Chinese revolutionary leader Mao Tse-Tung, 'is to study those laws for directing a war that govern a war situation as a whole. The task of the science of campaigns and the science of tactics is to study those laws for directing a war that govern a partial situation.'[47] Mao was writing about his guerrilla war against the ruling Chinese Nationalist Party (Kuomintang), but his words are relevant to all forms of warfare, for success or failure in war depends on how tactics relate to strategy and how strategy relates to war as a whole. The point of distinguishing between the fighting (known also in Clausewitz's *On War* as the 'engagement') and the strategy is to reinforce the rational nature of war, which, ultimately, is aimed at bringing about peace.

Strategy

At this stage it is appropriate to make a distinction between the principal levels of war. These are: strategy, operations (also known as campaigning) and tactics. Taking strategy first, then, this can be further subdivided into grand strategy and military strategy. Grand strategy is formulated and overseen by the highest ranking political leaders, civil servants and soldiers, and, in international relations, serves to determine how states marshal the vast resources at their disposal. However, grand strategies are usually implemented by people at lower levels. In this way, all these levels – strategy, operations and tactics – work in concert to decide the outcome of war. It might even be said that, of the three levels, strategy is the most important, for in Clausewitz's immortal words, it makes 'use of the engagement for the purpose of the war'.[48] The key lesson here is that brilliance at the lower levels of war cannot compensate for a flawed strategy further up the chain of command. US military intervention in the Vietnam War (1965–73), the Iran–Iraq War (1980–8) and the first and second Gulf wars (1990–1 and 2003–11) demonstrate the truism that success in war is only guaranteed if competence at all levels is evident.[49] With this in mind, this chapter explores the relationship between strategy and tactics, in particular, and argues that only by adopting the right strategic approach can success in war be assured.

In general terms, strategy is the umbilical cord that connects policy to military tactics. It is a political process that can bring success or failure, victory or defeat, and, ultimately, either further conflict or peace. By itself military strategy can rarely service the grand strategic goal. In the case of grand strategy, states frequently try to wield military might and political, diplomatic, and economic power for the specific objective of securing the ends as laid down by the government of the day. In simple terms, grand strategy provides the plan by which states navigate their way through the international system. It shirks short-termism and instead makes bold assertions about the future, which are generally the product of the intellect and experience of its most talented minds. Strategy, in the way it is practised in war, argues Professor Colin S. Gray, is '*the use that is made of force and the threat of force for the ends of policy*'.[50]

The powerful influence of strategic ideas in war ought to be obvious, though this is not always the case. Strategist J. C. Wylie believed that 'too few men, including the men who had them, have recognized the controlling strategic concepts and theories hidden behind the glamor or the stench or the vivid, active drama of the war itself.'[51] Nevertheless, the 'fog of war' should not blind us to the fact that strategy, even though it is judged the preserve of political and military elites, really does matter. At its core lies a conundrum: how do we relate our stated end goals to the ways and means at our disposal? Should we prioritize one approach over another and, if so, how? Moreover, what is the difference between strategy and tactics?

THE SPANISH ARMADA (1588)

In one of the most famous attempted seaborne invasions in modern history, King Philip II of Spain mobilized a plethora of grand strategic resources at his disposal to defeat the English. Diplomacy, financial inducements, blackmail, economic pressure, deception and propaganda were all employed in what became a personal duel with Queen Elizabeth I. It was recognized at the time that the odds overwhelmingly favoured Spain but that in battle Philip could do little to control the elements of 'friction' and 'chance'. Although England was poorly equipped financially and militarily to resist a Spanish Armada, intelligence nonetheless gave the English a battle-winning edge that had enabled them to plan in advance for the eventuality of invasion. The interception of prisoners and letters between Philip and his envoys allowed Elizabeth's spymaster Sir Francis Walsingham to place a spy in the King's court, who gained access to what Philip referred to in his writings as 'the plan agreed' (*la traza establecida*), which included details of the key elements of Philip's grand strategy. By itself, intelligence could not win the battle and it would come down to fighting at sea to repel the invasion. In the end, the Spanish Armada of 130 ships was defeated by a combination of bad weather, rigidity in the monarchical system of government, difficulty in command and control, and, vitally, the destruction brought to bear on enemy vessels by Elizabeth's naval commanders. Throughout the 1590s the war with Spain continued in various forms, each side denied the opportunity to administer a crippling blow upon its enemy that would guarantee a decisive victory.

Historically, the concept of strategy can be traced back in time to the ancient Greek word Στράτήγος (*strātēgos*), which literally means 'general' (an army leader), though it has its firmest intellectual origins in the work of Thucydides (*c.* 460–395 BCE). In Thucydides' magisterial *History of the Peloponnesian War* (431 BCE) we find a speech by Hermocrates, son of the Syracusan Hermon, who informs the people of Sicily how, after a lengthy period of war, 'The fact is that one side thinks that the profits to be won outweigh the risks to be incurred, and the other side is ready to face danger rather than accept an immediate loss.'[52] The question of how best to turn the odds to one's advantage is, above all, a strategic one. That one might choose to outsmart one's opponent both on and off the battlefield had already been considered by Chinese military strategist Sun Tzu, writing in sixth to fifth centuries BCE, who said that 'what is of supreme importance in war is to attack the enemy's strategy.'[53] Sun Tzu's writings offer us a glimpse into the interaction between strategy and tactics and how they have been effectively harnessed in battle to produce a favourable outcome in war.

Nowadays, we must consider war as both a practical and a conceptual problem, a point reinforced by Clausewitz. 'The first, the supreme, the most far-reaching act of judgment that the statesman and commander have to make', he wrote, 'is to establish … the kind of war on which they are embarking; neither mistaking it for, nor trying to turn it into, something that is alien to its nature.'[54] There can be no better illustration of this than in the making of war. For example, on 7 December 1941, the Japanese launched a pre-emptive attack on the US naval base in Pearl Harbor, Hawaii. The Japanese fleet had hoped to strike a decisive blow against the United States armed forces and, therefore, placed considerable stock in its strategy of annihilation. For some military historians such as Tim Bean, 'the Japanese obsession with the single decisive battle, coupled with a misplaced faith in their seamen's fighting spirit, proved a poor basis for conducting a war against the overwhelming resources of the United States.'[55] For others, like H. P. Willmott, Japan was driven by the 'desire to secure for herself the markets and resources of eastern south-east Asia that she regarded as essential for her long-term security and status as a great power'. In the mutual hostility with the US that had arisen in the inter-war period, particularly with regard to racial antagonism, the Japanese submitted to the 'inevitability' of conflict and 'chose to fight rather than tamely submit to American dictation'.[56]

As the Japanese would discover to their cost, scoring a tactical success, by destroying over a dozen warships and 300 aeroplanes in a surprise attack that claimed the lives of over 2,500 people, merely provoked a military giant, which would soon prove it had both the capability and a better strategy to match an opponent that relied heavily on an operational battle plan, not a coherent grand strategy for how to win the war it had embarked upon. By turning the American people so resolutely against them, the Japanese demonstrated a palpable lack of the strategic vision that is essential to winning a war. Tokyo's earlier victory in the Russo-Japanese War of 1904–5 made it overconfident in its ability to defeat a more powerful opponent. The history of war is replete with similar examples of political and military leaders who believed they could wage limited war for limited gains, only to find themselves confronted by the prospect of unlimited, total war.

More generally, the Second World War reveals how conventional forces can come unstuck when senior commanders disagree with one another about how best to implement strategy. Perhaps one of the most relevant examples of this is in the performance of the German army – an organization that was militarily effective, was good at disseminating its hard-won military tactics quickly by way of doctrine, could draw on the most technologically advanced equipment, and, above all, had a high calibre of fighting men at its disposal. In short, the Germans were proficient at the tactical level of war, yet Germany's General Staff did not fully understand the operational level of war (i.e. how tactics are used in specific campaigns) and, therefore, was prone to waging war in a way that depended more on luck or accident than strategic design.

SOVIET MILITARY STRATEGY

The Bolsheviks that came to power in the October 1917 revolution were distrustful of the idea of a standing army. They were opposed to the notion of what they referred to, pejoratively, as 'Bonapartism', which was the elevation of military technical leaders above revolutionary political leaders. In the face of an uneasy peace carved out between Germany and Russia in March 1918, the first commander of the Red Army, Leon Trotsky, claimed the Bolsheviks needed to build a revolutionary army using former Tsarist officers. The political commissar system was created to ensure military decisions were made in a way that was consistent with the Communist outlook. Unsurprisingly, this led to a conflict between commanders and commissars because of the level of political interference in operational matters. Trotsky himself favoured the military professionals, famously declaring that 'to play chess "according to Marx" is altogether impossible, just as it is impossible to wage war "according to Marx".'[57] In line with many of his senior commanders, Trotsky believed that Clausewitz, not Marx, illuminated the one true path military strategists ought to take, something that would be reflected in Soviet strategy making right up until the end of the Cold War.

The invasion of Russia by German forces in the summer of 1941 is another classic example of how Hitler's immersion in the day-to-day running of military campaigns left his professional officers' corps without recourse to challenge their supreme leader about his decisions. He simply usurped them whenever they disagreed with his orders and took command of the army himself in December 1941. Hitler's fanatical belief that he needed to destroy Bolshevism led him to make unwise strategic decisions, such as his launch of the attack on the Soviet Union. His tendency to micromanage military matters in a way that counter-manded the German army's High Command meant he was less likely to alter course when he committed troops to battle. Hitler's reluctance to relinquish centralized control over the armed forces ultimately aggravated frictions in command that would become more pronounced as the war progressed. By the time Allied forces landed in Normandy in June 1944, Hitler's policy of divide and rule had seen him suppress plans for a unified command in France, thereby effectively crippling decision making in the field and paving the way for Germany's eventual defeat.

In today's complex world, good strategy making in democracies is thought to be the product of due political consideration and sound military advice, something lacking in totalitarian states. Even so, there have been instances where this ideal relationship had its difficulties. The Western intervention in Afghanistan (2001–14) is hardly ever regarded as a success in strategy making. Planning for the war was haphazard and mired in confusion, and political and military leaders were unable to appreciate the kind of society in which they were operating. One of the biggest deficiencies Western militaries faced was the failure to understand their opponents. General Stanley McChrystal served as the senior US general in Afghanistan between 2009 and 2010. He was tasked by President Obama with looking again at the US Coalition's strategy and recalibrating it. In considering his options, McChrystal felt the US had two strategies it could adopt. The first was a counter terrorist approach, which would target key nodes (i.e. the Taliban's political, military and financial structures) and inflict a crippling blow on the enemy, and the second was a counter-insurgency approach that emphasized winning over the population in a more holistic way.[58] In the end, McChrystal recommended the latter course of action and President Obama subsequently accepted the military advice he was given. McChrystal's reputation for taking an unconventional approach to the business of war, however, was later to prove his undoing. In misjudged comments attributed to his staff officers, General McChrystal was accused of criticizing the Obama administration for indecisiveness. He promptly resigned and was replaced by General David Petraeus.

Procrastination in strategy making is almost as fatal as misunderstanding the enemy one is fighting. One of the biggest defeats of the Second World War came with the fall of Singapore in 1942. Considered a fortress in British colonial Asia (which also encompassed Burma and Malaya), the island was protected by huge artillery installations, which made it 'one of the most heavily defended pieces of territory in the British Empire'.[59] The eight-week battle involved 140,000 British and Commonwealth troops (9,000 of whom were killed and 130,000 taken prisoner) against three Japanese divisions numbering only 55,000 men, of whom 3,500 were killed.

Lieutenant General Arthur Percival headed up the Malaya campaign. While an experienced commander, he nonetheless faced a supremely intelligent, ruthless and determined opponent in General Yamashita Tomoyuki. In early December 1941, Yamashita launched an attack with a large naval contingent comprising twenty-four transport ships, which were carrying a total of three divisions of troops. The Japanese general was confident that his invasion of Singapore would be successful, primarily because the Germans had previously sunk a British ship, SS *Automedon*, which was carrying intelligence appraisals to the British general staff, exposing the weaknesses in the defence of the island. In formulating his military strategy, Yamashita was driven by two factors – the urgency of defeating British imperialist forces and the real possibility that, if he failed, he would have to commit ritual suicide, rather than return to Japan. In his bid to plug the gap created by a lack of numerical superiority, Yamashita ordered his troops to attack in large human waves. His whole plan hinged on the overwhelming speed and aggression of his troops, and within days Japanese forces had succeeded in capturing the island of Singapore, their main objective, well before British reserves arrived to relieve their beleaguered comrades.

The truth was that the determination of Allied troops mattered little when it became obvious on 11 February that the Japanese had totally encircled the island. Under instructions from his high command to fight to the last man, Field Marshal Archibald Wavell signalled Percival to inform him that it was at his discretion if he wished to 'cease resistance', which happened with a formal surrender on 15 February. In the end, the successful invasion of Singapore was attributed to sound military considerations having been taken into account by the Japanese. They correctly understood that their enemy lacked reserves and sufficient air power, and had only a scratch assortment of naval units at their disposal. With these disadvantages the new American-British-Dutch-Australian Command in Java could do little to resist Japanese offensive thrusts, especially when Allied defences had crumbled so easily. Yamashita had also succeeded, perhaps most importantly of all, because of the accuracy of his intelligence, the fighting spirit of his forces, and, above all, the correct military strategy.

What the fall of Singapore illustrates is that the paramount questions of strategy both at sea and on land turn on what naval strategist Julian Corbett calls the 'relative possibilities of offensive and defensive, and upon the relative proportions in which each should enter into our plan of war'.[60] Ultimately, the struggle for command of the sea, directly or indirectly, is the overarching concern of those who fight wars. They must ensure that they either accomplish this or at the very least prevent the enemy from doing so. If the aim of war is to seize something from the enemy, as in the case of Iraq's invasion and occupation of Kuwait in 1990–1, then it can be said to be offensive. Conversely, if the aim of war is to prevent one belligerent from taking something from another, such as the ill-fated defence of the Alamo in 1836, which was a siege in the ultimately successful Texan war of independence with Mexico, then the war can be said to be defensive.

Offensive and defensive strategies are not mutually exclusive but complementary, a point illustrated by the Russo–Japanese War. Then, the Japanese were concerned with the absorption of Korea into the Russian Empire and sought to invade and occupy the Korean Peninsula to prevent this from happening. At this time it was the audacious and ruthless initial attack by the Japanese that led to one of the most renowned naval victories in history.

Tactics

While strategies explain why wars are being fought (such as defeating the enemy or protecting one's state or territory from attack), tactics are the means by which human beings fight wars, including how they use weapons, such as swords, spears, tanks, rockets and machine guns, in battle to gain the advantage over their opponents. To paraphrase Clausewitz, tactics teach us '*the use of armed forces in the engagement*', while strategy determines how '*the use of engagements*' is linked to '*the object of the war*'.[61] In order to be successful in war, commanders have to ensure that they maintain momentum so as to accomplish the overall strategic goals as dictated by policy. The amphibious and airborne landings on D-Day, 6 June 1944, in the French coastal region of Normandy, provide a good example of how tactics matter to the overall direction of a campaign. Although the heavy bombers sent ahead of the main invasion force were meant to weaken the German occupiers' beach defences, they failed to knock out those situated along the water's edge. Much would now depend on the hard-won tactical lessons learned elsewhere and passed on in training to those who would make the landings, for most of these troops were 'green' and had not seen combat before. Captured in the haunting photographs of Robert Capa and Lee Miller, and, much later, in the popular movie *Saving Private Ryan* (1998), the landings on one beach alone, codenamed OMAHA, saw some 2,000 men killed before they even made it off the shoreline. Although it proved exceptionally costly, the Allied operation was successful in breaching the German defences, and by the day after D-Day the majority of the seaborne landing force (33,000 troops) had made it ashore.

The need to combine human willpower and determination with the capacity to deliver tactical success in battle had proven vital to the Allied war effort throughout the Second World War. Four years before D-Day, in the much-celebrated 'Battle of Britain' of August–September 1940, the German air force (Luftwaffe) was tasked by Adolf Hitler with breaking the will to resist of the British people prior to his planned invasion of the United Kingdom, known as Operation Sea Lion. According to military historian Antony Beevor, the massive mobilization of German planes included 656 Messerschmitt 109 fighters; 168 Me 110 twin-engined fighters; 769 Dornier, Heinkel and Junkers 88 bombers; and 316 Ju 87 Stuka dive-bombers. The British RAF had only 504 Hurricanes and Spitfires at their disposal.[62] The German military strategy was to destroy the RAF and also to choke Britain's war production by hitting factories, ports and radar stations. By mid-August the first large-scale attacks on British targets were launched. Pilots defending UK airspace showed remarkable courage and determination, even if they were heavily outnumbered.

Tactically, the RAF sought to break up the bombers with the Hurricane aircraft while Spitfires engaged enemy fighter aircraft.[63] RAF Fighter Command was, however, divided over tactics. Some favoured the so-called 'big wing' approach which pitted swarms of aircraft against the enemy head on, while others looked to smaller co ordinated attacks. One of the biggest disadvantages for the Germans was their inability to sustain this air campaign in the face of mounting losses. In fact, it would not be until June 1943 that German factories were fully capable of churning out 1,100 fighter planes every month, with production only reaching its peak towards the end of the war in September

1944, when output increased to some 3,700 aircraft per month. By May 1944 the Germans had lost air superiority over Europe and within weeks the Allied landings in Normandy would clear the way for the invasion of north-west Europe.

Technologically advanced weapons, equipment and, above all, imaginative tactics have proven invaluable in turning the tide in war. This was certainly the case in the Battle of Omdurman near Khartoum in 1898. There, the British army, small but well equipped with powerful gunboats and the newly invented Maxim gun, fought a Sudanese militia force several times bigger, and relying upon much older weapons. In the British mission to quell a rebellion led by a self-proclaimed Mahdi, Abdullah al-Taashi, the operational commander, General Horatio Herbert Kitchener, emerged victorious, having capitalized on his enemy's weaknesses and the edge his tactical superiority gave him. It was not without some justification that Winston Churchill could later write that the Battle of Omdurman 'was the climax and the final curtain of Victorian colonial war and the kind of leadership and tactics it produced'.[64] In all, 11,000 of al-Taashi's troops were killed in comparison to only 48 British and Egyptian soldiers.

These illustrative case studies bring the question of technology in war into much sharper focus. To be sure, the battle-winning edge afforded by technology and tactical innovation in war frequently emerges as the result of problems encountered by the modern state in its search for decisive victory, and it has its roots in the rise of industrialization from the late nineteenth century onwards. If we take, for example, the growth of railways, we can see how civilian benefits were inadvertently accrued by the military development of a massive network of rail tracks across the United States. In the 1830s only 9,000 miles of track had been laid across America; thirty years later the figure had trebled, thanks to the need to improve the logistical supply chain to front-line troops.[65] Technological advances matter in war, especially where it is thought that tactics provide the greatest advantage when confronting a determined and well-equipped enemy.

LEONARDO DA VINCI AND THE EVOLUTION
OF THE WEAPONS OF WAR

Leonardo da Vinci was one of the earliest designers of weapons of war. He held the title of Military Engineer under the Duke of Milan for fourteen years in the fourteenth century, famously designing tanks, breech-loading cannons, rifled firearms, wheellock pistols, rapid-fire catapults, balloons and flying machines. Hundreds of years ahead of their time, these machines never made it off the drawing board. However, da Vinci was merely following in the footsteps of the famous Greek mathematician Archimedes who had developed the catapult when his city, Syracuse, was threatened by the Romans in 215 BCE. It was the invention of the catapult that would start battle-winning technology off with a giant leap in what became a somewhat protracted development of battlefield weapons. We know that many of these inventions came about because of what has been called the 'Revolution in Military Affairs'. It began with fortification and siege warfare after 4300 BCE, bronze arms and armour after 3300 BCE, and the development of a disciplined force sometime between then and 2450 BCE. By 900 BCE, mass iron-armed infantry forces began to appear, to say nothing of chariots which were introduced into warfare in 2000 BCE.

Tactical prowess depends very much on the expert organization of military forces. In ancient Rome, the emphasis in battle switched from single combat between individual fighters, which was a 'means for the individual to win some glory for himself and ... to perform some services for the state',[66] to the collective engagement between larger formations, the professionalism of which was based on a clearly understood chain of command. After the Middle Ages, warfare became less the preserve of mercenaries enlisted on an ad hoc basis and more the preserve of standing armies. Under reforms initiated by Maurice of Nassau, *Stadholder* (military commander) of the Dutch armies in the late sixteenth century, the transformation of fighting from individualistic, single-combat engagements into collective enterprises – underpinned by drill and a recognizable chain of command – became 'real' and 'lasting'.[67] The organization of militias into regular armies, however, was not without its difficulties. Nevertheless, there was a movement towards routinization of tactics in training, with developments such as the reduction in the number of words needed to command men to load and fire muskets being an obvious instance of how technological innovation drove tactics.

The use of mass tactics in war would not come until the rise of modern industrialized warfare at the turn of the twentieth century. Training for soldiers had advanced considerably since the seventeenth century and soldiers were now organized into militias drawn from specific geographic areas. The British Army's regimental system eventually evolved out of these militias and would come to represent an effective means of enforcing discipline at the tactical level, enabling sub-units, known as battalions (i.e. forces of up to 800–1,000 soldiers), essentially to form the tip of a spear. By the First World War, battalions comprised four companies (120 soldiers each), which in turn comprised four platoons (thirty soldiers each), which, in turn again, comprised four sections (eight soldiers each). These battalions were now being deployed to concentrate mass and firepower on the battlefield. As one British Army aide-memoire made clear:

> The rifle and the bayonet is the weapon upon which every soldier must learn to rely both for attack and defence. Confidence in the bayonet carries men to the assault; confidence in the bullet beats off the counter-attack. These two are not separate, but one. The bullet supports the bayonet by covering fire; the bayonet completes what the bullet begins. The principle of the combined use of the rifle, namely, that the advance of any body of troops to the assault is covered by the fire of another body, lies at the root of all infantry tactics, and is known briefly as 'fire covering movement'.[68]

In the First World War, the British led the way in implementing a tactical plan centring on the principle of 'the artillery conquers and the infantry occupies'.[69]

This approach of wearing down the enemy by sustained force – which is known as attrition – would work only if there was sufficient numbers of guns and high explosive shells. In the case of the famed Battle of the Somme, which began on 1 July 1916, the British lacked the basic firepower necessary to degrade the German front line. By sheltering in a series of trenches and dugouts, the Germans were able to emerge relatively unscathed from the bombardment. The British Expeditionary Force Commander-in-Chief Field Marshal Douglas Haig 'made matters worse', according to military historian Gary Sheffield, 'by ordering the guns to fire on a large number of targets across the depth of German defences rather than concentrating fire on key areas'.[70] When soldiers from the thirteen British infantry divisions crossed the start line of their advance, they met with stiff opposition and thousands of miles of barbed wire and other battlefield obstacles. In order to free them up to traverse such obstacles, while closing with the enemy in order to seize and hold ground, one formation, the 36th (Ulster) Division, employed tactics similar to those which the French and German armies had also relied upon for success in battle. Realizing that tactics needed to evolve so as to minimize what J. F. C. Fuller called the submergence of the 'enemy's frontiers under a veritable inundation of flesh',[71] British artillery and infantry became more integrated as a result of an improvement in doctrine and technology by the end of the war in 1918.

Despite its obvious disadvantages in the First World War, attrition had reasserted itself as an integral part of the conduct of war at all levels. In the Iran–Iraq War, the human wave tactics of the Iranian Basiji units reinforced the view that martyrdom awaited those who had the courage of their convictions to advance towards enemy positions, often across minefields and against heavy machine-gun fire. Although these tactics served to conserve ammunition, it made it difficult for senior military commanders to lead the various regular and irregular components of the Iranian armed forces in a coordinated fashion. Nonetheless, when combined with significant pre-planning and innovative infantry tactics, the Iranians clearly held the upper hand during the offensive, even if the Iraqis proved particularly skilful at fortifying their defensive positions. In the Iranian offensive of January–February 1987, Tehran turned its attention towards capturing the southern Iraqi city of Basra, incurring massive casualties of 20,000 dead and 35,000 wounded. In total, 50,000 troops had been lost in attempting to take Basra during the war. In the end, mass, materiel and tactical improvement and innovation counted for very little in the face of inadequate strategy making higher up the chain of command. The Iran–Iraq War also exposed how the use of chemical weapons and the failure of the United States to continue its support for Saddam Hussein threw the lack of a real strategy into sharp relief.

Linking means to ends reflects the Clausewitzian adage that the purpose of fighting might well be to compel our enemy to do our will, but it amounts to little if it cannot be translated into clear policy gains. In doing so, though, strategists must also ensure that they remain flexible in the face of resistance from their opponents. In the examples considered above, it has been suggested that success in battle does not always translate into success in war, for to be truly effective in war one must ensure that strategy should always connect policy to tactics.

3

Regular war

Regular war is fought between the armed forces of states of a similar size and shape that use conventional military tactics and weaponry on a clearly demarcated battlefield. In contrast to irregular war, those who fight regular wars are often evenly matched, wear uniforms to distinguish friend from foe, and normally draw upon the support – direct and indirect – of all of the civilian population of their respective states. What does regular war look like? Its key characteristics are set-piece engagements between rival armies, which have encompassed everything from battles between horse-drawn charioteers in Roman times to the sailors who fought in the Russo-Japanese War (1904–5) and beyond, to the tank on tank warfare that came to characterize the Battle of Kursk (1943) and the clashes between Israeli and Egyptian pilots in the skies above the Sinai Peninsula in the Yom Kippur War (1973).

Although regular war has become synonymous with the modern industrial warfare that arrived with the clash between the great powers in the First World War (1914–18), it has antecedents in ancient times. Regular war rose to prominence in the years after the formation of the modern state, which is usually dated back to the time of the Thirty Years' War (1618–48). Some historians, however, emphasize the more modern pedigree of regular war, seeing it as having inextricable links to the modern state and being conducted principally between states, not within them (though there are exceptions) and having risen to prominence with the Industrial Revolution of the nineteenth century. In the orthodox understanding of this type of war, there is a clear distinction between the uniformed armed forces and the civilian population. The latter remain dependent on the former for protection, while the former depend on the latter for the financing and provision of weapons systems, ranging from rifles and grenades to howitzers and tanks, aircraft and battleships.

The naval historian Admiral H. W. Richmond was a champion of the state-based interpretation of regular war, describing it as 'a course of action to attain a national object – the object for which the nation went to war'. In asking the deceptively simple question, 'What is that object?', he argued that the object was 'to compel the enemy nation to compliance, to force them to accept a solution of some difference against their will'.[72] It is in the act of compelling an enemy to do something against their will that we see how states are uniquely placed to escalate violence to greater proportions than non-state actors, such as terrorist or insurgent groups, whenever the need arises. In regular war it is the government that is responsible for doing what it deems necessary to win the war, which usually means the mobilization of all of the physical, moral and conceptual resources at its disposal to conduct the war effectively. In the case of total war, governments deploy political rhetoric to persuade their populations of the dire consequences that defeat in war can bring, such as the physical destruction of the state itself, thus ensuring their compliance, consent and support for the war effort.

Clausewitz likened the fighting in regular war to a pair of wrestlers, evenly matched in physical prowess, each attempting to throw the other. Here he was suggesting that in order to win, each side must seek the total disarmament of his opponent's forces on land, at sea and in the air, all of which may be required to secure a decisive victory in war. In order to bring this about in practical terms, states must commit themselves to seizing territory, toppling rival governments and, in certain cases, subjugating whole peoples, to prove that they have won the bout. This might sound straightforward but it is important to acknowledge that there are constraints on the state's ability to win, such as the interplay of chance, friction (i.e. chaos) and the passion of one's enemies. All of these factors and more can very readily turn ambitions for victory into defeat or, most problematically of all, a set of unintended consequences of using military force that may make the objective and purpose of war elusive.

Total war

'Total war' refers to the idea that everyone in a state – the government, its armed forces and the people – is involved in a violent struggle to the finish, the outcome of which, if it ends in defeat, may lead to the annihilation of the state and its citizens. Although he did not use the term 'total war' himself, Clausewitz did go some way to defining 'the absolute character of war', which he equated with the campaigns of Napoleon Bonaparte in the late eighteenth and early nineteenth centuries. 'War, in his hands, was waged without respite until the enemy succumbed, and the counterblows were struck with almost equal energy,' the Prussian philosopher of war wrote of Napoleon.[73] This was a fight to the finish and the prize for Napoleon, according to Clausewitz, was peace, 'the only rational war aim he could set himself'.[74] Professor Chris Bellamy makes the case that we can see elements of Clausewitz's idea of absolute war (what would become known as total war) most readily in the war on the Eastern Front during the Second World War, when the belligerents waived all moral and legal restraints in order to fight perhaps the 'greatest, most costly and most brutal war on land in human history'.[75] Unimaginable horrors, however, grew in scale as the Allies realized that they could not inflict a decisive victory on their opponents without strategic bombing of civilian populations as a means of breaking the will of the German and Japanese governments to resist.

In seeking to break the resistance, the escalation of military operations led to huge battles – such as Stalingrad and Kursk – that could only be won with the full participation of the respective civilian populations in Germany and Russia. For German general Erich Ludendorff, who was in many ways the father of the concept of total war, the homeland was 'not only the basis on which our proud military power rested' but also 'the life-giving source which had to be kept clear, pure and yet potent, lest it lose anything of that virtue wherewith it steeled the nerves and renewed the strength of the Army and Navy'.[76] Ludendorff came to see Germany's defeat in the First World War not only as the failure of the army physically to break the enemy's will to resist, but also as a moral failure on the part of the German government and a large chunk of the nation. They had 'never yet understood the character of modern warfare', he complained, 'which demands the devotion of all its resources'.[77] European historian Tony Judt has argued that Israel has managed to achieve this since its formation in 1948 by keeping its citizens in a state of suspended animation, where the 'home front' has become almost synonymous with the 'war front' in what amounts to a 'politically calculated rhetorical strategy'.[78] Total wars, therefore, have far-reaching consequences for those who fight in them.

The onset of industrialized warfare, mass conscription and the need to mobilize whole populations in support of the war effort meant that governments, particularly in democratic societies, have tended to portray their enemies in a negative light. In the Pacific campaign of the Second World War, as we saw in chapter 1, race-based theories gained considerable traction in representing the enemy as demonic and subhuman. Unsurprisingly, propaganda has played a key role in generating feelings of an existential threat to ordinary citizens. Perhaps the most effective use of propagandistic sloganeering and ritualism ever employed by a state in total war was in Nazi Germany (1933–45).

The recognition that total wars require sacrifices by everyone in the state was not without its drawbacks, insofar as it became difficult to distinguish between who was a lawful combatant in the fighting and who was not. It is said that the American Civil War (1861–5) was one of the first modern industrial wars to mobilize all of the resources at a state's disposal. It saw huge set-piece battles between the Union and Confederate armies who utilized artillery, Gatling guns and bayonet charges and, in the words of one historian, combined 'the indiscriminate killing of mechanized war with hand-to-hand combat' in a 'vast butchery'.[79] The result was the deaths of 623,000 people on both sides and the wounding of 471,000, a massive number of casualties in a country with a population of only thirty million. The American Civil War was fought in a relatively short space of time and involved goals that its principal protagonists believed could only be achieved by the total destruction of the other side.

The American Civil War heralded the beginnings of what would come to be known as International Humanitarian Law, when President Abraham Lincoln asked jurist Francis Lieber to draw up a code that would safeguard the rights of armies and civilians. Building on the work of seventeenth-century Dutch jurist Hugo Grotius, who accepted that it was futile to try to eliminate war from everyday life, Lieber developed the idea of basic humanity (such as the rights of non-combatants, women and children not to be attacked in war) on the battlefield and urged restraint on those responsible for waging war. The Lieber Code (1863) would come to have some influence on the way the US fought regular wars at home and overseas. Nevertheless, it must be said that the burning of Georgia and the Carolinas by General Sherman in 1864–5 demonstrates the difficulty even states face in universally implementing ideas of restraint amongst their armies.

PRE-EMPTIVE VS. PREVENTIVE WAR

The attacks on the United States on 11 September 2001 illustrate at once the ease and the difficulty of interpreting International Law in terms of legalizing the use of force in the post-Cold War world. As a direct consequence, the US claimed it was acting in self-defence when, one month later, it took action against the Taliban regime in Afghanistan that sheltered the al-Qaeda terrorist group. However, considerable doubt still remains over the legality and legitimacy of the US-led campaign to topple Saddam Hussein in 2003, which is often seen as a consequence of President Bush's attempts to use military force against all threats, even ones that could not be directly linked to the terrorist attacks on 11 September 2001. The invasion of Iraq points to the dangers of a loose interpretation of the UN Charter and International Law in a way that emphasizes prevention as a legitimate means of dealing with security challenges. The following extract from the US National Security Strategy (2002) attests to this:

> The United States has long maintained the option of pre-emptive actions to counter a sufficient threat to our national security. The greater the threat, the greater is the risk of inaction – and the more compelling the case for taking *anticipatory action to defend ourselves*, even if uncertainty remains as to the time and place of the enemy's attack. To forestall or prevent such hostile acts by our adversaries, the United States will, if necessary, act preemptively.[80]

In this way, the US justified its pre-emptive invasion of Iraq by claiming it was designed to prevent further chaos through the proliferation of weapons of mass destruction (WMDs), which it believed Saddam had in his possession. Ultimately, though, such weapons were never found in Iraq.

Limited war

Limited war can be regarded as the opposite of total war – in that the survival of the state and its people is not in question – but the scale of the devastation, the intensity and the effects on the combatants can be just as significant. In naval warfare, victory is the principal means by which states can facilitate command of the sea and explains why the Battle of the Atlantic was one of the longest campaigns of the Second World War, particularly since victory must be fought for again and again before a decisive winner emerges. In the summer of 1770, the Russian Baltic Fleet dealt a decisive blow against the Turks by ambushing them off the coast of Asia Minor. A contemporary account recalls how the Russians 'kept pouring on them such showers of cannon balls, shells and small shot, that none of the many thousands of their weeping friends on land, who saw their distress, dared venture to their relief'. The crushing blows inflicted on the Turkish fleet, however, were insufficient to allow the Russians to 'consolidate their success', largely because of their stretched lines of communication, lack of bases along the Mediterranean and 'the simple facts of geography'.[81] The inability to defeat an enemy in limited wars like this one can still have tremendous consequences for the longer-term prosperity and security of states.

Air power, like sea power, can play an important role in regular war. In the Kosovo War (1999), aircraft gave the North Atlantic Treaty Organization (NATO) the ability to strike specific targets with precision. Codenamed Operation Allied Force, the sixteen-strong NATO alliance embarked on a bombing campaign aimed at dissuading the Yugoslav president Slobodan Milosevic from continuing his policy of ethnic cleansing against Kosovar Albanians who were seeking autonomy from the Serbian dictator. This was only one of a number of separatist ethnic conflicts that had broken out in Eastern Europe in the aftermath of the Cold War, when ethnic groups began to seek national self-determination as the former Republic of Yugoslavia (FRY) started to fragment. After seventy-eight days of devastating air attacks, and with the growing threat of a ground invasion by Western troops, Serbian forces withdrew from Kosovo and Milosevic was pushed to the negotiating table. In the process, NATO had incurred no casualties, though they did inflict some 5,000 casualties on Serbian forces while launching a staggering 38,000 sorties against pre selected targets, 10,484 of them attack sorties.[82] Throughout the campaign NATO commanders remained divided over what targets they should attack, agreeing to General Wesley Clark's three-phase operation, firstly, to bomb defensive positions and command-and-control centres; secondly, to attack infrastructural targets; and finally, to bring the war to Milosevic's door in his capital city, Belgrade.

THE AEROPLANE IN BATTLE

The aeroplane was first used in battle a few years prior to the start of the First World War. The Italians introduced it into their Tripoli campaign of 1911–12, as did the Bulgarian Army in 1912–13. Military commanders favoured it for its ability to provide accurate reconnaissance of enemy positions. However, it became indispensable by the outbreak of the First World War in 1914. The Germans had 200 planes in their fleet, more than twice the number held by the British and French armies, and it was to prove useful in both the surveillance and destruction of enemy positions. In his influential book, *The Command of the Air* (1920), Italian strategist Giulio Douhet argued that, rather than shoot down aircraft in the air, it was better to destroy the enemy's air force on the ground – by wiping out airports, supply bases and centres of production – so as to prevent them from sending planes up in the first place, thereby gaining air supremacy. Command of the air, in Douhet's memorable phrase, meant having 'the ability to fly against an enemy so as to injure him, while he has been deprived of the power to do likewise'.[84] Douhet's ideas were extremely influential in the development of independent air forces by the time of the Second World War. These could operate on strategic-level missions to penetrate enemy airspace and destroy targets, such as factories and other installations, vital for sustaining a war effort.

The strategy pursued by NATO was risky, though ultimately successful. The NATO secretary general at the time, George Robertson, referred to the victory in Kosovo as a 'defining moment' in European history precisely because air strikes were the 'quickest and surest means of disrupting violence in Kosovo'.[83] However, even the positive political effect this limited war produced for NATO could not hide the dangers of waging war by coalition. Then, NATO numbered only sixteen member states (it numbered twenty-eight in 2016), all of which had to agree by consensus how to fight the war. By the time of NATO's intervention in Libya in 2011, the dependency of the alliance on US military command and control and armaments was obvious.

Air power has proven important in other regular wars too. In the Falklands War between Argentina and Britain, which broke out after Argentinian forces invaded South Georgia and the Falkland Islands on 2 April 1982 in a bid to reclaim sovereignty over the British territories, aircraft were used to gain advantages in battle. The Argentine Air Force (FAA) sought to take command of the air by dispatching an assortment of aircraft – including Pucará ground-attack aircraft, Canberra bombers and Mirage III fighter jets – against the Royal Navy's Fleet Air Arm. In the Battle of Goose Green (28–9 May), Argentine aircraft mostly attacked tactically irrelevant parts of the British force, causing little damage. However, the British used three of their Harrier jump jets – in short supply during the battle – to strike perhaps one of the most decisive blows on their enemy in the entire ten-week war. Despite the use of aircraft at important junctures in the campaign, the Falklands War was predominantly a naval battle, with decisive victories also won on land. The use of air power in the Falklands War came at a price for Argentinian and British aircrews. The FAA incurred a total of 102 casualties (fifty-five men killed in action) out of a total number of 1,703 casualties (including 635 killed in action) and around 117 (Argentina placed the figure at fifty-nine) aircraft lost. The British figures amounted to 253 men killed in action and 575 wounded, with a comparative number of aircraft lost and airmen killed and wounded in battle.[85]

The Falklands War ended with the surrender of Argentine forces on 14 June 1982. At this point 10,000 Argentine troops had been amassed in Port Stanley in a last-ditch effort to defend the capital against the imminent attack by the British Task Force. By now, however, the morale of Argentine troops had flatlined and they were increasingly reluctant to continue fighting, particularly after some bloody land battles against British soldiers. A message to Admiral John Fieldhouse from the senior British land forces commander on the ground, Major General Jeremy Moore, carried news of the crumbling of Argentinian defences. The Argentinian troops reportedly threw down their arms and surrendered. The Argentinian commander, Brigadier General Mario Menéndez, quickly contacted his commander-in-chief, Leopoldo Galtieri, to request permission to enter into formal negotiations with the British to end the war, which took place at one minute to midnight. The Falklands War demonstrated what could be achieved by higher morale amongst fighting troops and the political will to see the job through until the end, regardless of the resistance offered by the enemy. It was an example of a limited war – in the sense that it posed no threat to the national survival of either state and was constrained by geography and resources – fought for the limited aim of seeking the withdrawal of Argentine forces in accordance with UN Security Resolution 502. It also demonstrated Prime Minister Margaret Thatcher's resolve that the people of the Falklands should be free to 'determine their own way of life and future'.[86]

How regular wars are fought

Regular wars have been fought in various ways – from the attritional trench warfare of the First World War, which witnessed mass armies try to wear down their enemies with overwhelming force, to manoeuvre warfare, which drew on close coordination between aeroplanes and tanks in the Second World War. The concepts of attrition and manoeuvre became integral to the fighting of wars around this time. This form of warfare was characterized by vast trench systems, tunnels and opposing armies facing off against one another across 'no man's land', with heavy guns sending men cowering into escarpments for cover from the bombardments. By 1916, the German military high command had shifted their strategy from seeking to inflict a single knock-out blow on the French in a war of annihilation, which is predicated on the assumption that a knock-out blow, or series of interlinked blows, could produce victory, to one of attrition, which, it was thought, would force France to the negotiating table more definitively. Professor William Philpott informs us that the two key attritional battles of 1916 – Verdun and the Somme – were 'not separate engagements but the two components of a sustained campaign of attrition' in which everything that 'happened in one battle had consequences for the other'. Verdun, he writes, demonstrated more clearly perhaps how industrial mass warfare could be 'intensive, slow, grinding and attritional by nature'.[87]

TANK WARFARE: THE BATTLE OF CAMBRAI, NOVEMBER 1917

The Battle of Cambrai in northern France was the first large-scale employment of the tank. In a coordinated attack on German positions along the Hindenburg Line on 20 November 1917, the British sent forward 378 tanks, supported by over 1,000 artillery guns and units from the Royal Flying Corps, which dropped bombs on German airfields, headquarters, artillery and machine-gun positions. The British took 4,000 prisoners in the morning and advanced some four miles by the end of the day, but the cohesion was effectively broken by desperate resistance from German gun batteries dug in at Flesquières Ridge. Further operations involving tanks over the next few days were unsuccessful, largely due to the loss of surprise, and a massive German counter offensive on 30 November ensured that the Battle of Cambrai ended in a 'draw'. The significance of Cambrai lay in the German failure to realize the true potential of the tank, something, twenty years later during the Second World War, they had learned and would employ readily to secure important strategic victories.

By the Second World War, however, attrition had become an intrinsic part of war, despite being a long-drawn-out and costly way (both in terms of blood and resources) of obtaining victory. The D-Day landings in Normandy in June 1944 involved the largest invasion force ever deployed in the history of warfare. By now, the war, which had commenced in September 1939, was moving towards an endgame as Allied armies mounted a daring attempt to breach German-occupied western Europe. In the early hours of 6 June, 1,200 planes dropped some 24,000 American, British and Canadian troops behind enemy lines. Their task was to seize bridges, disable German guns and secure positions along the coast ahead of the main invasion force, which had set sail the previous night.

The Battle of Normandy illustrates how the integration of land, sea and air forces, in a multi national coalition, can make a difference to the outcome of a campaign. However, it also proves that even though strategists in London and Washington wished to avoid long-drawn-out battles characteristic of the First World War, the enemy could not always be defeated quickly or easily. A vigorous counter-attack by the senior German commander in Normandy, Field Marshal Erwin Rommel, saw the Germans move onto the strategic defence in the hope that they could frustrate the Allies until reinforcements could arrive. The ambitious plan of the senior British commander, General Bernard Law Montgomery, to capture the strategic northern French city of Caen, hung in the balance. 'The struggle for Caen bogged down into a grim, bitter and protracted battle of attrition that lasted for six weeks,' remarked historian Russell A. Hart.[88]

If we take a look at how that war played out at a tactical level, we can see the difficulties that attritional warfare throws up for those who have to close with and kill the enemy. Although there was a lack of heavy opposition on the beaches where British soldiers landed, the light beach defences betrayed a much more elaborate set of defences further inland. If we look closely at the experience of the British 3rd (Infantry) Division, comprising almost 30,000 troops, which was tasked with taking the major city of Caen, we see that on the afternoon of 6 June 1944 they ran into stiff opposition from German 12th SS Panzer and 21st Panzer (tank) units in the forest enveloping the small town of Cambes-en-Plaine. The Division's spearhead battalion, the 2nd Battalion Royal Ulster Rifles, comprising some 750 troops, was the first to run into the German defenders of the town. They suffered heavy casualties in the attack, an outcome that demonstrated how well placed the Germans had been. Two days later the Royal Ulster Rifles launched a successful attack on the German positions, again incurring heavy casualties of eleven officers and 182 other ranks either killed, wounded, evacuated or missing in action. The attempt to break through enemy lines and thereby capture Caen had only a small chance of success in operational terms, because of the ability of the Germans to counter-attack even though they had been placed on the back foot by the invasion.[89] The failure by the Allies to consolidate the foothold in and around Caen illustrates how difficult it can be in attrition-based warfare to 'throw' an opponent in regular war.

What the fighting in this part of Normandy also exemplifies is Clausewitz's recommendation that the best strategy is 'always to be very strong; first in general, and then at the decisive point'[90] so as to punch a hole through the enemy's defensive position. At this particular stage in the battle for Normandy, the success of a second attack by the Ulster Rifles depended not only on the concentration of firepower and mass but on the enemy's decision to reinforce its lines along a much greater stretch of land. Therefore, it was the enemy's dispersal that made the advance by the Western Allies in that particular part of Normandy difficult.

FROM THE MUSKET TO THE AK-47

The development of weaponry has had a significant impact on warfare. Although slow to materialize up until the nineteenth century, a range of weapons from the catapult and longbow to the musket have made huge differences to the conduct of war. When it was first introduced onto the battlefield, the musket was unreliable beyond fifty yards and could only be fired three times a minute by a well-trained body of soldiers. Smaller arms, like pistols, were even less dependable beyond distances of twenty-five yards. It was not until the twentieth century that the self-loading rifle made an appearance. Referred to by former British foreign secretary Robin Cook as 'the real weapon of mass destruction', one of the most famous assault rifles is the AK-47, invented by Soviet military designer Mikhail Kalashnikov in the final days of the Second World War.

Born in 1919, Kalashnikov joined the Red Army in 1938, serving as a tank driver and a mechanic. He began work on a prototype of an assault rifle in 1942 and, after two failed attempts, he won the Main Artillery Directorate competition in 1945. The AK-47 entered service with the Soviet armed forces in 1948, earning Kalashnikov the coveted Order of the Red Star and the Stalin Prize. Today, his assault rifle, also known as the Kalashnikov, remains the most popular ever invented. Of the more than 500 million firearms in the world, at least 100 million are thought to be AK-47s.[91] As Kalashnikov later said of his invention: 'The weapon that I created and that bears my name lives its own life, independent of my life and my desires. Of course, when I see Bin Laden on television with his Kalashnikov, I'm disgusted, but what can I do about it? Terrorists aren't stupid: they too choose the most reliable weapons!'[92]

The need to remain mobile in the face of enemy resistance has been true of war since the time of Sun Tzu, who taught that nothing 'is more difficult than the art of manoeuvre', though it came to dominate thinking on regular war by the late twentieth century. From the Second World War, armies began to invest more heavily in manoeuvre as a means of avoiding being bogged down in static positions. As with other forms of regular warfare, manoeuvre stressed the need to organize troop movements to gain a favourable position in order to hit the enemy with a crushing blow. In *The Art of War* the emphasis is on deceiving the enemy, capitalizing and exploiting terrain, remaining 'swift' in order to 'move like a thunderbolt'.[93]

Examples of manoeuvre in war are not difficult to find. On 1 September 1939, five German armies invaded Poland in a coordinated plan of attack that was given the name Blitz-krieg (meaning 'lightning war'), a form of mechanized (usually soldiers accompanied by wheeled or tracked vehicles, such as tanks or lightly armed vehicles) warfare in which tanks and aeroplanes would be used to devastating effect in a series of bold attacks that outpaced and outgunned a stunned Polish opposition. The use of a combined attack had come a long way since the First World War, but it was in the employment of the aeroplane in a more offensive role alongside land forces that gave the German invasion its most devastating characteristic. By May 1940 German panzers had invaded France in close coordination with the air force, capturing some 1.8 million French prisoners, despite the French possessing more tanks, lightly armed tracked vehicles and artillery guns than the Germans. This attack emphasized how military leaders in France, Poland and elsewhere had failed to grasp the significance of this new way of war. General Ritter von Thoma, one of the most famous of the German panzer leaders, later gave military historian Sir Basil Liddell Hart five reasons for their success, which comprised overwhelming firepower concentrated on the weakest points; employing the element of surprise, such as night attacks; German air superiority; the ability of units to be reinforced with airborne parachute drops; and a first-rate logistical supply chain to sustain the ground troops.[94] In the end, however, it was the lack of a comprehensive strategy for war, rather than the adequate military strategy, that was to prove fatal for Germany and end in defeat in 1945.

In all of these forms of warfare, the state has remained central to the process, having mobilized its vast armies and populations to accomplish the goals set out by its politicians. Some scholars have suggested that Clausewitz's trinitarian concept of war, which combines bloodshed with chance and, paradoxically, the subordination of the means to political ends, reached its apogee during the first half of the twentieth century, and that this was reflected in the monopoly the state enjoyed for over a century in making war. The steady decline of Western influence, money and power has led scholars and policy makers reluctantly to conclude that there will probably be a shift in the balance of power in international relations towards rising and emerging powers in the east, such as China. This power transition will probably have a direct bearing on how we understand the changing character of war, away from the 'total war' concept of mass industrial armies holding and taking territory.

THE COLD WAR AND NUCLEAR WEAPONS

The Cold War began in the late 1940s when Soviet Russia moved to entrench its control over parts of eastern Germany. Although Winston Churchill had warned of an 'iron curtain descending over Europe' in 1946, it was the development of nuclear weapons by the Soviet Union in 1949 that opened the way for confrontation between the United States and its allies and the Soviet Union and its satellite states. In 1961 the crisis over Soviet intercontinental ballistic missiles deployed to Cuba escalated, raising the temperature so significantly that the scenario of the Cold War becoming a 'Hot War' was only narrowly avoided.

At the time the United States dropped its nuclear bombs on Hiroshima and Nagasaki, it was the only state to have developed the technology. Since 1945 that number has risen to nine and now includes the United Kingdom, France, China, Russia, North Korea, India, Pakistan and Israel. There are two types of nuclear proliferation. The first is vertical proliferation. Common during the Cold War, this was used to describe a limited number of state actors acquiring nuclear weapons, most famously when the United States and Soviet Union entered into an arms race. The second form of nuclear proliferation is horizontal. That is when multiple state, and potentially non-state (i.e. terrorist groups), actors acquire nuclear weapons. In strategic terms it is generally believed that a balance of power between states will guarantee stability of the international system, and that the risks and costs of using nuclear weapons are so high that rational state actors will not use them. However, this has also meant that governments can threaten the use of nuclear weapons to extract concessions. This is called deterrence and is believed to operate when governments not only possess nuclear weapons but signal to the world that they are prepared to use them.

The end of the Cold War was thought to have heralded the end of war in the capital cities of the powers caught up on the front line of the confrontation. The fall of the Berlin Wall, when it came, had enormous repercussions not only for international security but also for regional and state security. In London, the then Assistant Chief of the General Staff, Roger Wheeler, was watching events in Eastern Europe unfold from the Ministry of Defence headquarters:

The Secretary of State at the time used to talk about 'smaller but better', 'a peace divided', 'there isn't ever going to be another war', which, looking at what has happened since, is a strange thing to have said. And bear in mind, for the previous 30 years or so we'd been entirely fixed in Central Europe ... (except for Northern Ireland) and we had not really been in anything else. We had withdrawn from East of Suez in the 1960s ... And just before I arrived in July 1990 ... the Defence Policy Staff had written a paper trying to establish what it was that we [i.e. the Armed Forces] were [being trained and equipped] for now that the Soviet Union had gone away. And the senior civil servant in the Ministry of Defence wrote in response to this paper on 23 July 1990 'can anybody seriously imagine a British Prime Minister standing up in the House of Commons to announce a military adventure in the Middle East with the dispatch of an armoured division to the Gulf – what nonsense' … By 10th December that year – less than 6 months later – General Rupert Smith was commanding a division in the Gulf.[95]

Regular war did not end with the fall of the Berlin Wall. Wars in the Gulf, Eastern Europe and Sub-Saharan Africa since then have ensured that, while not now the dominant form of warfare, regular wars have not altogether disappeared. For General Sir Rupert Smith, industrial war between states has indeed become an endangered species and it is more likely that war will be fought in a very different way than it was at the turn of the twentieth century. In his words, 'War amongst the people is conducted best as an intelligence and information operation, not as one of manoeuvre and attrition in the manner of industrial war.'[96] The next chapter on irregular war queries the basis of this claim. This chapter has made the case that we must think of regular war in terms of the parity between opponents rather than the popular interpretation of it as a twentieth-century phenomenon. As we saw in several of the illustrative examples above, armies engage in a 'duel on a larger scale' and seek to strike a decisive blow at their enemy. Although the urgency appears to be at the operational level of employing force, it is still important to understand that strategy remains the deciding factor in warfare. By taking into account the change in the character of war, not its nature (which remains fundamentally unaltered), it is possible to ensure that we always keep in the forefront of our minds the utility of Clausewitz's trinity.

4

Irregular war

It was in 54 BCE when the famous Roman general Julius Caesar led an expedition to the remote and mysterious island of Britain. Despite adverse weather, the Romans managed to haul ashore most of the 600 ships and twenty-eight war galleys in their vast armada. As troops moved inland from the beaches, they were attacked by the local chieftain, Cassivellaunus, leader of the Britons. Quickly realizing the enormity of the invasion force mounted against him, Cassivellaunus moved to avoid a head-on clash with his superior and more technologically advanced opponent, thereafter resorting to guerrilla warfare in a bid to draw away the powerful Roman cavalry. As the Roman soldiers rode off in pursuit of the tribesmen, they inadvertently opened up their flank to a ruse that would allow the Britons to exploit their intimate knowledge of the physical terrain. Seeing an opportunity, Cassivellaunus simultaneously dispatched smaller raiding parties to pick off supply convoys. Caesar's army was promptly caught in an ambush. By adopting raiding tactics, the Britons proved that they could turn their lack of numbers and heavy cavalry to their advantage.

Historians would later observe how Roman legions frequently encountered 'people so barbaric and out of swim of current correct military procedure that they preferred skirmishing in the hills to the conventional set battle'[97] as they conquered lands as far north as the English Channel. The disadvantages facing the Romans would come to be faced by countless other technically proficient armies down through the years. The nature of their training emphasized set-piece battles with enemies cast in their own image. Once they realized that this could not hold under all circumstances, the Roman command structure and unit cohesion broke down. Legionaries quickly realized that this clever asymmetric challenge from their weaker opponents necessitated the adaptation of their traditional fighting style. A shift in tactics from forming a huge human 'battering ram' to being more individualistic on the battlefield soon followed. The classic phalanx formation – composed of 5,000 men, sixteen ranks deep, who overlapped their shields and pointed their swords and *pila* (javelins) in all-round defence – was eventually replaced by a looser fighting style. Roman troops could now freely engage their enemies on a one-to-one basis. Irregular war, then, is when two or more sides are engaged in a fight that recognizes the limitations as well as the strengths of their enemies and exploits this for strategic success. In contrast to regular war, where both sides are equally matched, irregular war can best be thought of in light of the biblical tale of 'David and Goliath', where a weak opponent fights a strong opponent but exploits the power differential to their advantage. David strikes Goliath in his weakest spot, thereby defeating him.

Throughout this period the Romans remained reasonably conservative in their responses to the changing character of war. Despite their caution, they did innovate in the face of an evolution in tactics. As was typical of classical warfare, Roman combat had several key characteristics, ranging from the prolonged duration of clashes, which were often decided over a period of three to five hours before one side broke and ran, to the high number of casualties amongst the vanquished. Roman infantrymen became highly mobile as their tactics adapted to the changing character of war, and they soon developed the concept of holding

troops in reserve, a military technique that permitted commanders to reinforce the front line as troops were wounded or became
tired. The history of the Roman conquest of north-west Europe
demonstrates that small groups of warriors turning to guerrilla
tactics can be successful, even when the odds appear to be stacked
against them.

Despite this long history of guerrilla warfare, it became fash-
ionable once again, in the wake of the Western intervention
in Iraq and Afghanistan in the early years of the twenty-first
century, to see irregular war as something entirely new and
novel. Nevertheless, as the opening vignette attests, this new
form of warfare represents a continuation of asymmetric tactics,
whereby opponents recognize their own limitations but also
those of their enemy and seek to exploit the latter. What is
innovative about the way in which these tactics are employed
in war today, however, is the increasing turn towards hybridity, which demonstrates a blurring of the regular and irregular boundaries in war. In hybrid warfare, regular forces quickly
reconfigure their organizations to integrate a range of regular
and irregular capabilities. Well-established examples include the
militant groups Saddam Fedayeen in post-2003 Iraq, Hezbollah
in Southern Lebanon, the Tamil Tigers in Sri Lanka, and Daesh
in Syria and Iraq. All of these groups boasted an array of weapon
systems, from rifles through to rockets, and mixed and matched
tactics to attack their enemies, using synchronized suicide bomb
attacks, coordinated guerrilla assaults and rockets fired into fixed
enemy positions.

Similar mix-and-match tactics of hybrid warfare have also
been utilized by states. In 2014 Russia began to deploy unmarked
forces in Ukraine to undermine the authority of the pro-European
government in Kiev. The insertion of Russian Special Forces troops
(known in the media as 'little green men') into the country saw the
Russians promptly encircle key strategic Ukrainian military bases,

undermine international law and place the West on the back foot. Leaders in Washington, London, Paris and Berlin were taken by surprise by the innovative Russian hybrid strategy. In reality, as the next chapter will demonstrate, there is nothing 'new' in this form of war – it is simply the clever blending of regular and irregular forms of warfare by strategists.[99] In war, as in life, some things change but other things stay the same (*plus ça change, plus c'est la même chose*), and, with this in mind, it is important to recognize that the essence of irregular war remains marked more by continuity than change.

HYBRID WARFARE

The term 'hybrid warfare' was first coined by the US Marine Corps in the 1990s. It is the point at which the conduct of war becomes blurred so that it is difficult to tell the difference between regular war and irregular war. Hybrid warfare also suggests that those who turn to this way of war are usually cognizant of their own strategic and tactical limitations, or have detected these in their enemies. As one of its principal proponents, Lieutenant Colonel Frank Hoffman (Ret'd) argues that hybridity in war represents a blurring of the different types of war (regular, irregular and terrorist) that can be practised by state and non-state actors alike. Examples of hybrid warfare vary and range from the Tamil Tiger terrorist group in Sri Lanka, which utilized a range of tactics from suicide bombing to air raids and attacks by fast boats on naval patrol vessels, to Daesh in Iraq and Syria, which has used guerrilla warfare, conventional weapons systems (tanks, armoured personnel carriers and UAVs (unmanned aerial vehicles, or drones)) and terrorist tactics, to Russian intervention in eastern Ukraine. For Hoffman, hybrid wars will continue to present us with 'a complex puzzle until the necessary adaptation occurs intellectually and institutionally'.[98] Despite some strategists, including Hoffman himself, suggesting that hybrid war is nothing new, his conceptualization is useful in understanding how war can adopt its own 'grammar' while reflecting the context in which it is waged.

Types of irregular war

Cyril Falls, a renowned Oxford Professor of the History of War, describes four types of irregular war, or what he calls 'small war'. The first is 'war against primitive peoples, most often colonial wars'; the second type is the 'guerrilla revolt against a government'; the third is 'a kind common in Latin America in which both sides are armed with up-to-date light weapons but virtually no heavy ones'; and the fourth is a more modern, 'entirely underground and secret warfare', which we would today call terrorism.[100] Each of these specific forms of small war bring to the fore the need for states to rise to the challenge posed by the armed groups who oppose them.

If we turn to the second category of 'small war', we can find ready examples of guerrilla armies crippling their much larger opponents by capitalizing on their weaknesses. As a major colonial power in the nineteenth century and into the twentieth century, Britain had considerable experience of waging small wars. Its experience of fighting nationalist-inspired insurgencies, however, was not always a positive one. One of the most resilient insurgencies involving Britain was in Southern Ireland during the Irish War of Independence of 1919–21. The 'Irish question' had long dogged British attempts to establish a form of self-government (known at the time as 'Home Rule') on the island. Indeed, the roots of armed insurrection against British rule extended all the way back to the United Irishmen, an anti-colonial movement founded in 1791. One hundred and twenty-five years later, another group of revolutionaries were attempting to overthrow British rule by seizing key buildings in Dublin, the Irish capital, during Easter week of 1916. They failed after a sustained bombardment by the British, which broke the cohesion of the uprising, though this defeat did not dampen Irish nationalist spirits and the struggle for independence continued unabated. Following the execution of the leaders of the Easter Rising, the Irish Republican Army

(IRA) began a clandestine terror campaign against the British that would culminate in guerrilla warfare a few years later. IRA leaders recognized that they could not hope to defeat their enemy in open battle and so looked to other methods to challenge them in more strategic ways.

One of those leaders who had evaded the firing squad in 1916 and who went on to become one of the most accomplished revolutionaries of the twentieth century was Michael Collins. Collins has since been credited with inflicting decisive victories that exploited the British inability to govern by consensus rather than coercion. 'On the Irish side it took the form of disarming the attackers,' he would later write. 'We took their arms and attacked their strongholds. We organized our army and met the armed patrols and military expeditions which were sent against us in the only possible way. We met them by an organized and bold guerrilla warfare.'[101] But this was not enough. Collins believed that to truly paralyse 'the British machine' it was necessary to assassinate key individuals responsible for administering and enforcing British rule in Ireland. 'Without her spies England was helpless,' wrote Collins. 'It was only by means of their accumulated and accumulating knowledge that the British machine could operate.'[102] The plan became more ruthless and sophisticated once the British doubled their numbers. In Collins's opinion, these reinforcements only made Britain more vulnerable:

> We struck at individuals, and by so doing we cut their lines of communication and we shook their morale. And we conducted the conflict, difficult as it was, with the *unequal terms* imposed by the enemy, as far as possible, according to the rules of war. Only the armed forces and the spies and criminal agents of the British Government were attacked. Prisoners of war were treated honourably and considerately, and were released after they had been disarmed.[103]

The insurrection was highly successful and forced the British to the negotiating table. As a result of talks in London, Ireland was partitioned into two separate jurisdictions in 1921. The British may have ceded control to a Dublin government but it would not be until 1949 that the Irish 'Free State' would declare itself an independent republic, free of British interference. The guerrilla war had demonstrated how weakness could be turned to strength in warfare. However, it also pointed to political limitations when it left the north-eastern part of the island under British control, which would precipitate further bloody conflict half a century later.

Another successful guerrilla campaign that appeared to mirror IRA tactics in Ireland was the Cuban revolutionary struggle of the 1950s. Led by the charismatic Communist leader Fidel Castro, the insurgents (known as *compañeros*) were vastly outnumbered and outgunned by the regular armed forces of the Cuban president General Fulgencio Batista. A law graduate from the University of Havana, Castro had intended to follow a political path until Batista overthrew the government and installed a military dictatorship. In 1956 Castro and his *compañeros* landed in Cuba and fought a two-and-a-half-year armed struggle that saw Batista's forces defeated and his regime overthrown. In his memoirs Castro explained how his militarily inexperienced irregulars fought a successful campaign against a much stronger and better-equipped enemy:

> We revolutionaries learned the art of war up there [in the Sierra Mountains] by fighting. We discovered that the enemy within its own positions is strong, but the enemy in motion is weak. A column of 300 men has the strength of the one or two platoons who lead it; the others don't fire in combat, or they just shoot in the air to make noise – they can't see the troops that are firing on their advance positions. That was one of the elementary

principles we used: attack the enemy when he's weakest and most vulnerable. If we attacked positions, we'd always have casualties, we'd waste ammunition, we wouldn't always take the objective; the enemy was dug in, so he could fight with more information and more safely. Little by little, our tactics evolved; I'm not going to talk about that, but we gradually learned to fight against a strong adversary, and Column I was our elementary school.[104]

GUERRILLA TACTICS

With the rise of civil wars after the end of the Second World War, the tactics adhered to by guerrilla groups have evolved. Peng Teh-huai, a senior commander in Mao Tse-Tung's Red Army, once told the journalist Edgar Snow that the fundamentals of guerrilla warfare were 'fearlessness, swiftness, intelligent planning, mobility, secrecy, and suddenness and determination in action'.[105] From 'hit and run' tactics, which rely on speed and aggression, to attacking the enemy at their 'weakest link', guerrillas have identified the weakness of stronger opponents since the formation of the modern state in the seventeenth century. By the second half of the twentieth century guerrillas combined well-established tactics with the acquisition of new technologies that have given rise to the relatively inexpensive construction of Improvised Explosive Devices (IEDs). Between 2011 and 2013 the number of Suicide Borne IEDs and Vehicle Borne IEDs used worldwide grew from 156 to 484 respectively. By 2014, Somalia, Libya and Nigeria were leading the way in terms of the number of fatalities inflicted by IEDs. Algeria and Mali accounted for the top five states afflicted by IED attacks in Africa, while Afghanistan, Iraq, Colombia, Pakistan and India are seeing more and more such attacks by guerrilla and terrorist groups.[106] The employment of IEDs is driven by the need of terrorists and insurgents to work with low-tech alternatives to the huge resources that states invest in countering these 'hit and run' tactics.

The intellectual foundations for Cuban guerrilla warfare had been laid by the Chinese Communist leader Mao Tse-Tung much earlier, in the 1930s. Mao believed that it was essential for the guerrilla to defeat a stronger opponent if the manpower provided by the population were harnessed to the ends of revolutionary war. The concept of establishing a firm base amongst the local population would come to define guerrilla warfare in the twentieth century and remain a constant feature of irregular war into the twenty-first century.

There is a sense, then, in which Cyril Falls's fourth type of small war, terrorism, has come to define the so-called 'new face of war' in the early twenty-first century. It has been said that 'war always involves violence, but not all violence can be described as a war.'[107] This is certainly true when we examine the challenge posed by terrorism to state security, which has grown exponentially since the end of the Cold War in 1991. A transformation in the means and methods utilized by terrorists was evident during the wars of decolonization in which European empires – from France and Portugal to Britain and Belgium – fought non-state groups that turned their emphasized ethno-national grievances and ideological sentiment into the substance required to fight protracted campaigns. The Provisional IRA, the Basque separatist group Euskadi Ta Askatasuna (ETA) and the Algerian Front de Libération Nationale (National Liberation Front, in English, or FLN) made natural bedfellows when it came to mounting terrorist campaigns against Britain, Spain and France.

With the fall of the Berlin Wall and the collapse of the Soviet Union, the creation of power vacuums in the Middle East, Sub-Saharan Africa and Eastern Europe led to the onset of new forms of terrorism, much less limited in their ideological goals. Suddenly, Iraq, Somalia and Afghanistan became bywords for Islamist terrorism and insurgency that threatened the national security of Western states which had believed that a 'peace dividend' would follow the lifting of the state-based threat of nuclear war. States now had to contend with a whole new set of non-state security challenges that became more transnational in scope, more unpredictable and more deadly than anything they had hitherto encountered.

THE RISE OF DAESH

The threat posed by Islamist terrorism came to the fore with the attacks on the United States on 11 September 2001. The subsequent invasion of Afghanistan in 2001 and Iraq in 2003 further fuelled the fire of Islamist insurgency and terrorism and led, in 2014, to the emergence of Daesh, a militant group that follows a toxic blend of extremist Wahhabi, Salafi and Takfiri doctrines from within Sunni Islam that advocate violence against non-believers. Daesh began life as Jama'at al-Tawhid wal-Jihad, a group that pledged allegiance to al-Qaeda and Osama bin Laden in 2004. After the death of its founder, Abu Musab al-Zarqawi, in 2006, it merged with other insurgent groups in Iraq to form the Islamic State of Iraq (ISI). Its aim was to establish an Islamic caliphate. When civil war broke out in Syria in 2011, it sent a mission to fight there, and became known as ISIS (Islamic State in Iraq and al Sham (the Arabic word for the Syrian region)). After an intense power struggle, al-Qaeda cut off ties with Daesh in 2014.

It is often said that al-Qaeda had its immediate roots in the Soviet intervention in Afghanistan between 1979 and 1989, and to an extent Daesh could be said to have its roots in the American invasion of Iraq between 2003 and 2011. What makes Daesh such a durable threat both in the Middle East and the West is not only its military prowess but also its alarming ability to harness the support of disaffected Sunni populations in Iraq, and the rest of the world.

Militarily, Daesh has employed a range of terrorist and insurgent tactics, such as mass executions of Iraqi and Syrian soldiers, policemen and civilians, and the kidnapping and beheading of journalists, aid workers and government officials, which maximized their coverage in the news and spread fear around the world. Daesh fighters have used tanks, artillery and even aircraft along with vast supplies of AK-47s, rocket-propelled grenades and an assortment of other small weapons. By holding ground in large cities in the Middle East, and carrying out 'punitive' and deadly attacks in countries like France in response to international attempts to quash the organization, Daesh has shown it is unlikely to be defeated in a conventional military sense any time soon.

Irregular war – a high-risk strategy for states

Irregular wars are often protracted affairs, usually drawing a state into prolonged conflict with smaller opponents who may use terrorism or insurgency as a means of extracting political concessions. Some of the most powerful states have encountered considerable friction in waging war against irregular adversaries since the end of the Second World War. One of the clearest cases of friction between state armies and guerrillas was the Soviet intervention in Afghanistan in the 1980s. Because of the deployment of front-line troops to the Central European Front in the early 1980s, conscripts came to form the backbone of Soviet forces in Afghanistan before regular troops could arrive. Soviet strategy and tactics altered from the deployment of infantry and heavy armour to the reorganization of formations into motorized infantry to give them more mobility in the often rugged and mountainous terrain. By 1980 Hind helicopter gunships began to fill the skies above Afghanistan, tracking and killing small knots of mujahideen fighters, in a bid to neutralize those resorting to ambushes. The purpose, as one journalist recalled, was to 'clear the land by aerial bombing, followed by airdropping of troops'. Alongside air mobility, Soviet forces also resorted to guerrilla tactics, with Western sources reporting how 'Cuban and Vietnamese advisers, experienced in such warfare, are said to be in Kabul to aid the Soviet Army.'[108]

With his accession to the General Secretaryship of the Communist Party, Mikhail Gorbachev sought to alter the strategic tempo of operations in Afghanistan, approving more intensive military pressure by expanding the Soviet mission in the country from 26,000 soldiers to 108,000. Russian troops now seized and held key population centres and lines of communication and undertook more aggressive military operations. Brute force was generally regarded as a reaction to the Communist failure to win the consent of the people they had originally claimed to be intervening to help. Coercive tactics included the dropping of bomblet mines from planes over populated areas, the rigging of children's toys with IEDs and the summary executions of villagers accused of aiding and abetting the mujahideen. Two Russian deserters who made their way to London seeking political asylum in 1984 revealed the extent of the brutality being meted out to Afghan civilians by the Soviet Army:

> The officer would decide to have the village searched and if it was found it contained a single bullet, the officer would say: 'This is a bandit village: it must be destroyed.' The men and young boys would be shot and the women and small children would be put in a separate room and killed with grenades.[109]

Although these techniques were redolent of the Red Army of the 1920s, the turn towards coercion by Soviet forces in Afghanistan underlines how desperate they had become to see an end to the fighting.

The former British diplomat and chronicler of Russian military intervention in Afghanistan, Rodric Braithwaite, suggests that in the wake of the major offensive in Kunar province in May–June 1985, the Russians 'moved away from massive ground operations towards more flexible actions in support of the Afghan army, backed where necessary by long-range bombers from Soviet territory'.[110] By the late 1980s the Soviets had begun to face severe structural problems, including bankruptcy and imperial overstretch, which would hasten the end of their military involvement in Afghanistan. In one of the final set-piece battles in the eastern city of Jalalabad, Soviet forces equipped their Afghan allies with a battery of Katyusha rockets and other modern heavy weapons. While over 3,000 missiles (including Scuds) were fired in the engagement, the mujahideen still managed to turn the tide of the war more generally in their favour. Sensing they were facing imminent defeat, some 500 government troops defected to the guerrillas, signalling the end of hostilities.[111] Like earlier anti-colonial struggles in Ireland, Cuba and Yemen, Afghanistan promptly descended into a long-drawn-out civil war until the Taliban seized control of the Afghan capital, Kabul, in 1996 and enforced a strict regime based on a literal interpretation of the Qur'an and the imposition of Sharia (Islamic) Law.

The Taliban would remain in power until the US intervened in the wake of the al-Qaeda attacks on 9/11. Operation Enduring Freedom saw US bomb attacks against Taliban bases and the routing of 50,000 Taliban troops outside Kabul at the beginning of October 2001. Within the space of a month the US military and their Northern Alliance allies had defeated the Taliban, leading to mass surrenders in Mazar-e-Sharif and Kandahar in early December. Approximately 8,000–12,000 Taliban fighters died in this phase of the war, with some 7,000 more taken prisoner. On 6 December the signing of the Bonn Agreement ended hostilities for the time being, though it was never seriously judged to be a peace accord since the losing side did not participate in the negotiations about the country's future. This would cause considerable problems further down the line, with Taliban and al-Qaeda fighters making good their escape to Pakistan. By operating from a veritable safe haven in Pakistan's Federally Administered Tribal Areas, the Taliban were able to regroup, reorganize and plot their revenge on the US-backed administration in Kabul.

By 2003 the Taliban had begun its guerrilla war offensive in the southern provinces of Kandahar, Zabul and Helmand, all nested on the border with Pakistan. Within twelve months the Taliban had initiated a full-scale insurgency, drawing on the almost endless revenue generated by the poppy-growing trade in the country. As a consequence, the international community agreed to back the Afghan government and an International Security Assistance Force (ISAF) was formed, drawing ground troops from over thirty-seven nations. The British, who had fought three previous wars in Afghanistan, were deployed to Helmand in southern Afghanistan, thought to be the toughest province in the country, to carry out counter terrorism and counter narcotics operations on behalf of the Afghan government.

In several districts infantry regiments had come to the country with considerable experience in counter-insurgency, but the most immediate problem was that they were spread thinly over an area the size of Wales with a population of approximately 100,000 people. The British Task Force, in contrast, initially numbered only 1,200 troops and could call on very few Afghan National Security Forces. A lack of cultural understanding, intelligence on the insurgents, training and education amongst the local security forces and the paucity of a discernible grand strategy from Washington and London prolonged the campaign. A new counter-insurgency campaign would not be in place until 2009–10, when senior US officer General Stanley McChrystal took command of the NATO-led mission. When NATO combat troops withdrew in 2014, the Taliban were still undefeated. By 2015 many countries, including the US and the UK, were redeploying small numbers of troops to augment the Afghan National Security Forces in their continued fight against the insurgents. The war that for Afghans began in the 1970s, if not earlier, appeared insoluble.

The role of intelligence

Afghanistan proved that overwhelming force and technological sophistication could be no match for a shrewd insurgent enemy. This was not the first time that this harsh lesson had been learned. The Vietnam War (1965–73) demonstrated that a lack of cultural understanding on the part of the United States, along with poor intelligence on guerrilla enemies, could be fatal. It demonstrated how even the wealthiest and most powerful nations on earth can quickly find their political ambitions defeated by an enemy pursuing an asymmetric strategy. Without question the 'one-war' strategy pursued by US general William Westmoreland to drive out North Vietnamese forces from South Vietnam was dependent on the massive bombing campaign by the US Air Force over North Vietnam. Although the Westmoreland years were seen to be heavy-handed, pacification operations were also carried out in rural parts of Vietnam. Nevertheless, these major operations came to rely heavily on intelligence to determine a much more vigorous anti-guerrilla approach. For commanders on the ground, this meant building up a more complete picture of their area of operations so as to more productively neutralize the insurgent.

In irregular war, intelligence is considered vital in building up an accurate picture, not only about how many personnel the enemy has at its disposal, but also how they are structured and armed, and, perhaps just as importantly, how well they have adapted to the physical and human terrain in which they operate. It is the latter point – human terrain – that lies at the heart of guerrilla warfare. As renowned Brazilian Communist Carlos Marighella once observed: 'Guerrilla war is an irregular war having nothing in common with conventional warfare, and therefore counts on assistance, shelter and sympathy from the people.'[112] Irregular war may denote a disparity between one belligerent and another, but it also begs the question of what it is that the weaker side are doing in order to close the gap and mount a convincing campaign against a (usually) bigger, stronger and better-equipped enemy.

Although the Vietnam War is considered a mainly American affair, it did also involve support from other nations. The 1st Australian Task Force (1ATF), numbering some 4,500 troops, was responsible for Phuoc Tuy Province, which bordered Cambodia. Their main enemies were units from the regular North Vietnamese Army and irregular Viet Cong (VC). The VC's modus operandi was typical of guerrilla movements in that it preferred to overrun training centres and bases in a bid to inflict heavy losses on the enemy. The pattern of mounting raiding operations, along similar lines to the guerrilla tactics employed by the Britons in 54 BCE, continued until January 1968 when they were beaten back by US forces and suffered heavy losses. Nonetheless, VC commanders continued to pursue large-scale ambush tactics.[113]

In order to tackle the threat, 1ATF changed its emphasis from conducting major operations (coercion) against the enemy to pacification (winning consent) of the local population. This new departure was announced in May 1969 but it lasted only six months, after which the US senior adviser ordered that pacification operations cease in favour of South Vietnamese units taking the lead.[114] With the introduction of Vietnamization from 1970, the Australian mission adapted to 'restore security in Phuoc Tuy and to develop the capabilities of the GVN [Government of the Republic of Vietnam, or South Vietnam] to maintain that security'.[115] In all, 500 Australian servicemen lost their lives in the Vietnam War and a further 3,000 were wounded. The deployment had mushroomed from thirty advisers in 1962 to a battalion-strength formation in 1965 and a task force of 4,500 by 1966.[116]

After 1973 the US military turned away from counter-insurgency. It was thought that the 'bad war' in Vietnam undermined the concept and distracted them from their mission of building up conventional forces. Nevertheless, in other parts of the world, militaries continued to find themselves engaged in fighting insurgencies. In Northern Ireland, the British Army had been deployed in 1969 to keep the peace between warring factions of Protestants and Catholics. By 1971 a rejuvenated IRA had emerged to take the fight to the British. Elsewhere, the Bangladesh Armed Forces had emerged from a war with Pakistan, fighting for revolutionary independence, only to have to re-engage an irregular enemy in the form of small knots of fighters sympathetic to Pakistan. By now modern war-fighting forces were being asked to perform policing functions that kept the protection of state interests at the heart of their strategic designs. Knowing that large-scale formations of troops faced harassment from smaller, nimbler groups of irregulars, states began to develop new Special Forces capabilities to counter the threat.

SPECIAL FORCES

Modern Special Forces have their origins in the Second World War. The best-known example was the British Long Range Desert Group, subsequently renamed the Special Air Service (SAS) Regiment, which operated in small, self-sufficient teams behind enemy lines. Like the Special Operations Executive (SOE), the SAS began life as a covert paramilitary unit that inserted itself behind enemy lines in order to fulfil strategic-level tasks, such as disabling enemy aircraft on the runway, blowing up installations and killing or capturing senior military, security and political figures. Since the 1940s almost every state has developed some kind of Special Forces capability. The rationale behind the employment of Special Forces was to give states a more agile edge to accomplish strategic objectives. The agility demonstrated by highly trained groups – in terms of offering long-range patrolling on foot over inhospitable terrain and the ability to work stealthily behind enemy lines – also gives states the opportunity to achieve strategic security objectives with a high degree of plausible deniability. However, Special Forces are also able to offer a multitude of advanced skills that most soldiers do not possess, such as languages, medical training to rival world-class surgeons, and a degree of confidence that makes them much less risk-averse than their regular counterparts.

In the 1950s and 1960s British Special Forces were heavily committed to assist in the management of British colonial campaigns. The SAS had learned much from their earlier involvement in Radfan operations in southern Yemen and were increasingly being tasked with dealing with the threat posed by terrorists and insurgents who turned to asymmetric strategies and tactics. Although they were known for their perfection of advanced infantry tactics, the SAS also pioneered insertion into hard-to-reach enemy territory by way of free-fall parachuting. One former SAS commanding officer said that the advantage of this tactic was that 'you could keep close together and more or less land close. There was one thing that always amazed me. We were very good navigators. We were very very accurate.'[117] Increasingly, the SAS were being employed whenever the British government required strategic-level intelligence; the sort of game-changing competitive edge that could be used to turn the tide on a range of state and non-state adversaries. In the 1960s this demand would increase in line with the competition between President Gamal Abdel Nasser, who was a key figure in the spread of the anti-colonialist pan-Arab movement, and the ailing British Empire, which supported monarchs across the Middle East.

The SAS worked in close cooperation with other branches of the British armed forces, including the Royal Air Force, to give them greater strategic reach and support in the world's harshest and most inhospitable terrain. Intelligence became a prerequisite for success on these covert operations and, as such, the SAS offered the British government plausible deniability. Little was known about the organization until May 1980, when black-clad SAS men stormed the Iranian Embassy in Princes Gate, London, and rescued hostages being held by gunmen from the Democratic Revolutionary Front for the Liberation of Arabistan. The soldiers involved in Operation Nimrod became heroes overnight and were to become mythologized in popular culture.

Special Forces emerged out of a tougher military culture in the United States after the defeat in Vietnam. The formation of 1st Special Forces Operational Detachment-Delta (known popularly as 'Delta Force') in the late 1970s was modelled on the SAS. As its founder and first commanding officer, Colonel Charlie Beckwith, noted, 'I knew in England I had stumbled upon a concept that, when welded with the American system, would improve many of the things we did in the Special Forces.'[118] It would take much longer for the concept of Special Forces to become accepted in US military culture, particularly after high-profile disasters such as the attempted Delta Force rescue of US hostages in Iran in April 1980. Nonetheless, as one former senior US general, Wesley Clark, would later admit:

> For the Special Operations Forces, a twenty-year effort toward legitimization reached fruition in Iraq. Outcast after Vietnam, discredited by scandal and elitism despite incredible accomplishments and bravery, the SOF community worked step by step to break down the barriers of security and mystique that precluded their full integration into the battlefield fight. In Panama, in Desert Storm, on the hilltops overlooking Kosovo, in Afghanistan, and now inside Iraq, they brought elite skills, courage, and a very small 'footprint' to battlefield success.[119]

The British SAS and American Delta Force have been much imitated around the world, with states as geographically diverse as Germany, Colombia, Saudi Arabia, Oman, Iraq and Afghanistan having the capacity to call upon these units to secure strategic advantage by way of covert action in a world where wars are increasingly becoming irregular in character.

Counter-insurgency and pacification

The rise of 'new wars' following the end of the Cold War was accompanied by a serious crisis amongst Western states about how to respond to complex and unpredictable threats. The belief that superiority in terms of technology and firepower could win any military engagement, including counter-insurgency (or COIN, as it would come to be known), became a substitute for really engaging with the problems thrown up by the alien environments in which most troops found themselves deployed. Far from a new set of techniques, tactics and procedures, COIN was a reinvention of a diverse range of methods used by European colonial powers as they beat a retreat from empire. Collectively this process was referred to by the British and French as 'pacification', wherein the political, economic and social process of establishing or re-establishing local government was seen as a process complementary to military activity aimed at defeating insurgents. Pacification included the provision of credible territorial security, the destruction of the enemy's capacity to provide an alternative to state authority, and the forcible construction of a contractual relationship between the government and the people.

By the early twenty-first century conventional armies were demonstrating an aversion to irregular warfare. 'Most of their doctrine, training, ethos, and experience reflect their preference for engaging in operations against enemies trained and armed more or less like themselves and for employing similar tactics', writes military historian Gregory Fremont-Barnes.[120] Notwithstanding the reality that counter-insurgency warfare is essentially a competition over power, one of the remarkable features of the new wars of the early twenty-first century – ergo Western intervention in Iraq and Afghanistan – was the predilection of military commanders to cherry-pick ill-fitting lessons from history as a way to guide them in their application of the use of force. Polaroid snapshots from the much-lauded British campaigns in Malaya in the 1950s, Aden in the 1960s and Northern Ireland in the 1970s were used as templates, rather than examples of how problems were solved according to timeless principles. This would have disastrous consequences and lead to the expenditure of much blood and treasure by the United States and United Kingdom.

In the irregular armed conflicts of the twenty-first century there has been an almost schizophrenic tendency to play up the utility of counter-insurgency tactics, while simultaneously denying that there is any continuity happening in war. While warfare – that is to say the conduct of war – has undoubtedly changed, there is much more continuity in war than commentators would like to admit. One critic of COIN, Colonel Gian Gentile, has gone as far as to suggest that this is merely a dangerous passing fad. 'Modern counterinsurgency', says Gentile, 'is age-old antiguerrilla warfare in new clothes.'[121] To an extent, this criticism is borne out by a cursory glance at the historical record, where the term 'counterinsurgency' was regarded as 'an odd and obscure word'.[122] However, as Colonel Alex Alderson has concluded, it is important also to remember that even though 'the strategic context in which they are applied has changed', this does not invalidate the lessons learned. 'The question is not whether broad principles are relevant', he argues, 'but the extent to which those principles of British doctrine have been followed, resourced, and applied.'[123]

Modern militaries have undergone a radical transformation over the past decade, which has seen them acquire a greater depth of understanding of the places in which they are likely to operate. This new-found situational awareness has been precipitated by the disappearance from view of the 'old certainties' of the Cold War and the advent of the 'age of uncertainty'. Now and in the future it is anticipated that 'new' irregular threats, like terrorism and insurgency, will pose an even greater challenge to global, regional and state stability than 'old' state-based conventional threats. In attempting to grapple with the conceptual repercussions of this paradigm shift, from inter-state wars to 'wars amongst the people', military practitioners have looked to a handful of innovative thinkers in their own ranks – as well as some civilian academics and consultants – to help them make sense of these profound changes in the global security environment. Unsurprisingly, militaries have arrived at the realization that in order to mitigate present and future challenges, they must be prepared to outsmart their adversaries mentally as well as physically.

Intellectual dissidents are rare within conservative institutions like the military. Where they have spoken out, they have bravely questioned the wisdom of meeting the challenge posed by irregular adversaries with a Cold War era mentality. Perhaps one of the most famous examples where this has happened and led to operational successes was in Iraq. And it came in the most unlikely form. General Stanley McChrystal, the commander of Special Operations Forces in the second Iraq War, explained how the transformation came about:

> Our organization was designed for a problem that no longer existed; we had brought an industrial age force to an information-age conflict. After several years working with leaders in private industry, I believe this same challenge confronts organizations in every sector of the modern environment. In previous generations, when organizational models resembled the orderly hierarchy I first drew on the whiteboard in Iraq, success depended largely on creating the most efficient bureaucratic model. But in the information age, when our streamlined hierarchy encountered a networked enemy, we found ourselves optimizing for variables that had become irrelevant, and we were immediately outpaced.[124]

In terms of radically rethinking the business of waging war in the twenty-first century, McChrystal made the case that al-Qaeda in Iraq was a networked threat that required an innovative networked response. This point was also being made in regular unit formations around the same time, with tactical-level innovation seen as the only viable means of seizing the advantage over adversaries who knew the ground better than the occupying power. For instance, a vehicle recognition system – similar to what the British used in counter terrorist operations in Northern Ireland – was put in place in order to monitor the movements of terrorists and insurgents. The 1st Battalion, 7th Marine Regiment (known as 1-7), applied Artificial Intelligence software from the Phoenix Police Department in the United States to 'simultaneously fuse information from multiple databases'[125] in their operations across al-Qaim. Significantly, those units which were largely equipped to deal with conventional warfighting demonstrated their organic abilities to adapt from the bottom up to the realities of the environment in which they found themselves operating.

There are, of course, examples of militaries failing to adapt to the changing context in which they find themselves battling irregular opponents. The Israeli withdrawal from the Gaza Strip and parts of the West Bank by the early twenty-first century came about according to some experts because of the 'unlikelihood of a conventional attack by Arab state armies'.[126] Historically, these territories had been occupied in the wake of the Six Day War of 1967 because they offered Israel 'strategic depth', but this no longer proved the case after the outbreak of the first intifada in the late 1980s. Twenty years later they were arguably proving a danger to Israeli national security. Israel's war with Hezbollah in 2006 has been singled out as an example of how an irregular enemy can very quickly do something completely unexpected by turning to conventional war and choosing to hold ground, firing salvos of rockets in an attempt to inflict heavy losses on state-based armed forces, and paralysing the Middle East's most technologically advanced army by adapting its strategy and tactics to exploit the weaknesses of its opponent.

Even if we regard as fanciful the popular argument that Israel lost the war primarily because of its dependency on superior firepower and technology, the outcome did at least create the impression that weaker non-state opponents could inflict serious defeats on states and their armed forces. The allure of US victories in the first Gulf War of 1991 and the Kosovo War of 1999 may have convinced Israel and other states of a need to rely on the Revolution in Military Affairs. The case of the 2006 war between Israel and Hezbollah demonstrates that, even with military superiority, states cannot hope to defeat an enemy, even an irregular one, without an adequate strategy that links tactics on the ground to policy goals. Without clear end goals, even the strongest of belligerents will find themselves in trouble.

The end of the Cold War had a huge impact on the security landscape. Not only had conventional wars become rarer, but there was an upsurge in the number of civil wars. A worrying trend identified by experts is that it has become increasingly likely that those places which have experienced some kind of war in the past are more likely to suffer a relapse at another point in the future. Unfortunately this has become more of a problem as Western states turn away from the concept of intervening in civil wars in regions as geographically far-flung as the Middle East, Sub-Saharan Africa and South-West Asia. This dependence on the West, though, has not ended and may yet have profound repercussions for how war develops in the future, as we will see in the next chapter.

5
Future war

The pattern of future war is difficult to predict with any certainty. Although the character of war changes over time and from conflict to conflict, we do know that its nature always stays the same. But, when future war is considered in any great depth by experts, they almost invariably focus on the technological advances, rather than the deeper question of what armed conflict will look like in ten, twenty or even fifty years' time. Even though it may be sensible to pay heed to the impact of technological developments in war, we also need to take stock of the intellectual challenges that accompany the changing character of war. In order to rise to what leading American strategist Peter Paret has called 'the cognitive challenge of war',[127] we might profitably ask what armed conflict is likely to look like beyond the '9/11 Wars' in Afghanistan and Iraq. The Italian military theorist Giulio Douhet argued that thinking about the changing character of war often requires us 'to make a mental excursion into the future'. Douhet recognized how the exercising of one's imagination during wartime was a crucial and 'ever-present practical necessity'.[128] But before we do so, it is important that we address two interlinked problems: first, is it actually true to say that the character of war has changed in recent years? Second, if it has changed, then does it also follow that we are equipped to deal with that change now, and in the future?

What does conflict look like at present?

As we discovered in the chapter on regular war, armed conflict is thought to have radically transformed since the end of the Cold War. We noted that Mary Kaldor and Rupert Smith both questioned the validity of old conceptualizations of war and warfare. Their argument was that 'old wars' between nation states no longer exist and that the continued use of the military to achieve policy goals – by itself – is ineffective in so-called 'new wars', which tend to be fought 'amongst the people'.[129] This critique has been largely accepted by Western states, which have sought to respond to these new and emerging challenges by shifting their understanding of force from discrete concepts of warfighting, peacekeeping and humanitarian operations to what are referred to variously as 'the three-block war', 'the future character of conflict' and 'the mosaic of conflict', all of which stress the importance of combining the military, economic, diplomatic and developmental instruments of power in pursuing policy by way of force. The bottom line in all of this debate and discussion about how war has changed appears to be that the global security picture is now considered more uncertain, more complex, more intertwined and more volatile than ever before.

Globalization has been one of the most important drivers underpinning this change in warfare. For the most part, states have recognized that globalization is a double-edged sword: while it offers opportunities, it also presents challenges in the form of security threats and risks. 'Hard' security threats, such as international terrorism, the proliferation of WMDs, failed states and transnational organized crime, have all contributed to greater instability. 'Soft' security threats and risks, like pandemic diseases, climate change, competition over energy and natural resources, poverty, inequality and poor governance, also now pose clear challenges for states, a pattern which is set to

THE THREE-BLOCK WAR

First conceived by the American general Charles Krulak in 1997, the three-block war suggests that modern militaries may well find themselves delivering humanitarian aid on one street, conducting peacekeeping/stabilization operations on another, and engaging in traditional warfare in yet another. A few years later another Marine, Lieutenant General James Mattis, suggested that a fourth block ought to be added, which zeroed in on information operations (i.e. the use of computing software to help create favourable conditions within which conventional forces could operate). This was something acknowledged by non-Western military theorists, including those in China, who have been talking up the prospects of informational war since the late 1990s, and the Russians, who had begun to put it into practice in Eastern Europe from 2007 onwards. The three-block war concept challenged how Western militaries thought about warfare, especially since they had been used to facing the prospect of either a conventional Soviet threat in the Cold War or a counter-insurgency operation against an irregular adversary. In these discrete military activities, states were prone to organize their armed forces in ways that matched likely opponents or challenges. After the end of the Cold War the US privileged new technologies over strategy with respect to traditional combat operations, and gave less thought to how it might also deal with the challenges of peacekeeping after 1991 or the emergence of new and more complex security challenges. The three-block war challenged these assumptions and paved the way for innovative thinking on warfare.

continue into the future. What makes these threats and risks all the more significant is that they often coexist and threaten to destabilize internal state cohesion, particularly in fragile, failing and failed states, where the risk of war is believed to be much greater.

It would be wrong to suggest that globalization is the only driver of this change. The transformation in the character of war is also the product of a range of other factors. These include the long-term consequences of the Cold War, whether that is directly attributable to the 'blowback' experienced by East and West in their manipulation of conflicts by proxy (i.e. the Vietnam War and the Afghanistan War), the rise in ethnic conflict within and beyond Europe, or the shift in power relations from West to East in the aftermath of the Cold War. This should not come as a complete surprise. Writing amidst the death pangs of the Soviet Union, Israeli military historian Martin Van Creveld warned:

> In the future, war will not be waged by armies but by groups whom we today call terrorists, guerrillas, bandits, and robbers, but who will undoubtedly hit on more formal titles to describe themselves. Their organizations are likely to be constructed on charismatic lines rather than institutional ones, and to be motivated less by 'professionalism' than by fanatical, ideologically based loyalties. While clearly subject to some kind of leadership with coercive powers at its disposal, that leadership will be hardly distinguishable from the organization as a whole; hence it will bear greater similarity to 'The Old Man of the Mountains' than to institutionalized government as the modern world has come to understand that term. While rooted in a 'population base' of some sort, that population probably will not be clearly separable either from its immediate neighbors or from those, always the minority, by whom most of the active fighting is done.[130]

The picture painted of future war in Van Creveld's seminal study *The Transformation of War* was certainly prescient. In many ways it predated the emergence of the type of irregular threats which came to prominence in the two decades after the end of the Cold War. As we were to witness in armed conflicts in Bosnia, Sudan and Iraq, these 'wars amongst the people' would see rival groups seek to exterminate their enemies along religious, ethnic, cultural and national lines.

It is also important to recognize that even though the drivers of war and the enemies changed, so too did the way in which wars were fought. In one of the most significant observations of the post-Cold War world, General Charles Krulak informed politicians on Capitol Hill in 1998 that:

> The threat of the early twenty-first century will not be the 'son of Desert Storm'; it will be the 'stepchild of Chechnya'. Our opponents will not be doctrinaire or predictable. They will not try to match us tank for tank and plane for plane in an attempt to fight the kind of Industrial Age war to which we are accustomed. Instead, they will seek to fight us where we are least able to bring our strength to bear. As recently seen in the bombing of our east African embassies, they will not limit their aggression to our uniformed military. Today we are witnessing only the tip of the iceberg. Combined with the proliferation of high-tech weapons and weapons of mass destruction – which further empower both 'third world' nations and non-state entities – this complex, dynamic, and asymmetric conflict might well be as lethal as a clash between superpowers. One thing is certain, this twenty-first-century threat will be far more difficult to manage.[131]

With the attacks on the United States on 9/11, the world was to witness how far war had been transformed in the minds of those unfettered by International Law or International Humanitarian Law. In the intervening years, Western governments have contin-ued to see the gravest threat to their national security coming from terrorist groups, rather than conventional armies. Interest-ingly, this is not the case in other parts of the world. Existen-tial threats to security are different depending on where you are situated, what you consider to be under threat (e.g. international, regional, state or human security) and the time period you are considering.

A large part of the equation in deciding what people consider to be a threat comes down to whether you believe yourself to be vulnerable to it. In South America, for example, transnational narco-cartels, economic crises and the challenge of anarchist or leftist terrorism tend to preoccupy government thinking in Buenos Aires, Bogotá and Santiago more readily than, say, Islamist terrorism or WMD proliferation. Elsewhere, in Sub-Saharan Africa, the prevalence of disease pandemics (HIV/AIDS, malaria and Ebola), together with limited access to clean water and, in some cases, the rise in militant Islam, tends to feature more highly on the agendas of governments. Twenty years ago, of course, this would have been different. In the South Pacific islands, the growing disconnection between rulers and ruled led to violent opposition demonstrations in Tonga, military coups in Fiji, and poor economic development exposed by natural disasters in the Solomon Islands. In South Asia, the presence of enormous populations coupled with disease, hunger and poor governance gives the impression that instability is actually the norm. In Bangladesh, the perennial issues of natural disasters, regional instability and political corruption have served to remind us of other security concerns that affect both state and human security.

It has been proven in recent years that the optimism greeting the end of the Cold War and the prospect of some kind of 'peace dividend' between states was somewhat premature. With the onset of conflict in the Caucasus, the Balkans and other parts of Eurasia, we have seen the resurgence of strong states that are prepared to use force to get their way. Similarly, weak states now act as an incubation chamber for extremism. The emergence of Daesh in Syria and Iraq from early 2014 serves as a warning that non-state actors do not play by the same rules as states when it comes to war. As we saw in the previous chapter, how states respond to these armed groups has a considerable bearing on their evolving strategy, tactics and even their performance on the battlefield, as well as in respect to future attempts to combat them. In a briefing to reporters at the Pentagon six months after the 9/11 attacks, Defense Secretary Donald Rumsfeld gave an insight into the difficulties faced by states as they seek to formulate strategies and responses to the myriad of threats now ranging against the West:

> Reports that say that something hasn't happened are always interesting to me, because as we know, there are known knowns; there are things we know we know. We also know there are known unknowns; that is to say we know there are some things we do not know. But there are also unknown unknowns – the ones we don't know we don't know. And if one looks throughout the history of our country and other free countries, it is the latter category that tend to be the difficult ones.[132]

With such a broad range of threats now present and emerging in the international system, it is perhaps prudent to turn to the question of whether we are actually equipped to deal with them.

Are we equipped to deal with twenty-first-century war?

If war has changed so much in the past quarter of a century, how then can we meet the challenge of adapting to future war as mapped out for us by esteemed theorists like Paret and Douhet? One answer might be to look to the past for clues about how and why things changed in earlier times. In thinking about how we might use history to light our path into the future, it is perhaps prudent to look at how some thinkers have made important leaps of faith in other non-military contexts. The inventor, entrepreneur and CEO of Apple Inc. Steve Jobs is quoted as saying:

> You can't connect the dots looking forward; you can only connect them looking backwards. So you have to trust that the dots will somehow connect in your future. You have to trust in something – your gut, destiny, life, karma, whatever. This approach has never let me down, and it has made all the difference in my life.[133]

Jobs's observation is interesting for it highlights how we must bridge the gap between what we know and what we don't yet know with something akin to 'gut instinct'. In war, the need to trust one's gut instinct – or, more precisely, one's intuition – is a risky business. For those making decisions that might mean the difference between life and death, this intuition must be based on sound experience, professional knowledge and, above all, the right strategy. Without at least a 'good enough' strategy, decisions in war will lack direction and we may even find it impossible to face the future with any kind of confidence or optimism. Having said that, we must realize that strategy remains more of an art than a science. It can certainly ensure that we are orientated in a better direction and may even help us challenge 'wishful thinking', while resisting the urge to misapply old logic to new problems. Leading strategist J. C. Wylie has argued that we can build firmer intellectual foundations for analysing future war if we think of strategy in both military and non-military terms. The idea of exerting control of 'one social entity over another', argued Wylie, is common to all power struggles and '[m]ilitary matters are inextricably woven into the whole social power fabric'.[134]

Leading strategic thinkers agree that if the 9/11 wars have taught defence and security professionals anything it is that strategy can be done better. It is worth just pausing here for a moment to remind ourselves of what is meant by strategy and how it can equip us to deal with conflict better. Strategy joins policy to tactics; it provides the plan by which we can orientate ourselves to the political and military environment around us. Strategy rejects short-termism in favour of bold assertions about the future and sweats the intellect of its most talented minds in a way that forces them to scan the horizon for risks, hazards and opportunities in a manner that can offer solutions to even the most complex or wicked of problems. The wars of the early twenty-first century demonstrate, quite clearly in fact, that a disproportionate amount of time has been spent looking for a template from past experience that might help meet the challenges of the present and future. This was certainly the case at the time of 9/11. Rather than heed the warning issued by Charles Krulak, state militaries, intelligence agencies and bureaucracies sought refuge in prior experience, and failed to forecast, even in general terms, emerging threats.

In the US government's 9/11 Commission report, published in the wake of the atrocities, it was noted that there had been a crippling failure in intelligence exploitation. In seeking to explain why this could have happened, experts clambered to announce the arrival of a new form of warfare, which was anti-Western (with extremist groups particularly opposed to what they saw as American interference in the Middle East), religiously inspired, and intent on inflicting mass casualties among both civilian and military populations. The US response to the attacks was predictable. The liberal commentator Christopher Hitchens captured it brilliantly:

> As I write, fighter planes are the only craft in the sky over New York and Washington, and indeed, the rest of the country. The National Guard is on the streets. The Atlantic and Pacific coasts are being ostentatiously patrolled by large and reassuring Navy vessels. Not only does this deployment do absolutely no good today (it

has about the same effect as the newly imposed ban on kerbside baggage check-in at airports), but it would have made absolutely no difference if it had started last Sunday … Yes, it does give the impression that we are 'at war', all right. But being on manoeuvres is not the same as warfare, and 'preparedness' and 'vigilance' are of little value if they contribute to the erection of a Maginot Line in the mind.[135]

The kind of conventional thinking that Hitchens was challenging, though, is not itself new. One has only to go back to the 1940s to the work of writer George Orwell to appreciate the dangers of faulty strategic thinking in relation to the threat posed by totalitarian regimes. In his essay 'Notes on Nationalism', written in the closing stages of the Second World War, Orwell warned that 'Political or military commentators, like astrologers, can survive almost any mistake, because their more devoted followers do not look to them for an appraisal of the facts but for the stimulation of nationalistic loyalties.'[136]

Orwell's ability to shine the powerful light of reason on questions of defence saw him divide military commentators into two camps – 'pro-blimp' and 'anti-blimp'. It was a clear nod to the Colonel Blimp cartoon character which first appeared in the London *Evening Standard* in the 1930s, a man who found himself out of sorts in a modern war he neither liked nor understood. Orwell saw the leading strategic theorists of the 1930s and 1940s – J. F. C. Fuller and Basil Liddell Hart – as representative of these two key trends inside England's political class at the time. He believed that both the left and the right in Britain were capable of reading whatever they wanted into the works of Fuller and Liddell Hart in a way that satisfied their deep-seated political or ideological biases. It is worth reflecting on Orwell's critique in light of the ongoing debate over the 'lessons' to be taken away from the '9/11 wars'. David Kilcullen has made this plea in relation to how we might apply these lessons to the challenges of future war:

> It's time for the generation who fought the war to take what they learned in the hills and valleys of a landlocked conflict, and apply it to a challenging new environment; it's time to think about the implications of the coming age of urban, networked, guerrilla war in the mega-slums and mega cities of a coastal planet. It's time to drag ourselves – body and mind – out of the mountains.[137]

In the wake of military campaigns in Iraq and Afghanistan, we have seen an exponential rise in context-specific lessons, rather than the development of problem-solving tools that can be applied to future situations. Most of those who advocate the sanctity of context-specific lessons are prone to emphasize change at the expense of continuity. Very few actually challenge conventional wisdom. This is to be expected in organizations, such as militaries, that are conservative in their outlook and tend to privilege group-think and obedience to authority above contrarianism. While it is necessary to maintain cohesion in organizations responsible for using lethal force, it also conspires to produce a rigidity in thinking and a tendency to avoid anything that might be construed as intellectual heresy. In a fast-paced, complex institution like war, it is little wonder that soldiers are more likely to erect a defensive wall, either physically or mentally – in Hitchens's phrase a 'Maginot Line in the mind' – than to deconstruct it.

Technology and the future direction of war

On 5 May 2011 two advanced Black Hawk stealth helicopters carrying US Special Operations Forces operators landed near a compound in Abbottabad, Pakistan. The men on board were tasked with the mission of killing or capturing the leader of al-Qaeda, Osama bin Laden, who had been tracked by intelligence agents in the months running up to the operation. According to some sources, the original plan was to target the compound in a drone strike, thereby eliminating the mastermind behind 9/11. As the planning for the operation progressed, it was finally decided to send in troops to ensure they got the right man and avoid unnecessary collateral damage. Despite one of the helicopters clipping the compound wall, resulting in it having to be abandoned, the operation was a success. All of the Special Forces operators made it safely back to their base just over the border in Afghanistan. Not long after the operation, American spies and Special Forces operators were in action again, this time in Yemen, where they targeted a convoy carrying a senior leader of al-Qaeda in the Arabian Peninsula (AQAP), Anwar al-Awlaki. He escaped, despite US forces firing repeatedly at his vehicle. UAVs again lacked the ability to deliver the decisive result senior counterterrorism officials in Washington so badly sought in their Global War on Terror.

On 30 September 2011, the United States succeeded in killing al-Awlaki and another US-born AQAP leader, Samir Khan, in a drone strike near Khashef, ninety miles north-east of the Yemeni capital Sana'a. The targeting and assassination of al-Awlaki was personally approved by President Obama and carried out by the highly clandestine CIA drone programme. The US believed al-Awlaki posed a significant threat to national security, in that he inspired individuals around the world to become involved in jihad. But serious questions have been raised about the strategic, ethical and moral decisions that have led Western states to engage their enemies far from the battlefield and by remote control (as with drone attacks), without recourse to the normal checks and balances one expects to find in liberal democracies.

The advances in technology since 9/11 have meant that aircraft can be flown by operators half a world away. Drone strikes are popular amongst the American public because they are seen to be relatively low in cost and result in fewer American casualties. Data are extremely difficult to come by because of the highly classified nature of the US drone programme, but the Bureau of Investigative Journalism has estimated that there have been somewhere in the region of 875 drone strikes in Pakistan, Afghanistan, Yemen and Somalia over the past decade. Approximately 5,752 suspected militants and 1,135 civilians have been killed in these attacks. The vast majority of these strikes occurred during President Obama's term in office.[138]

The idea that Islamist insurgents can be deterred from their extremism only through the application of hard power is a curious

Drone strikes in Yemen, Pakistan, Somalia and Afghanistan, c.2004–14

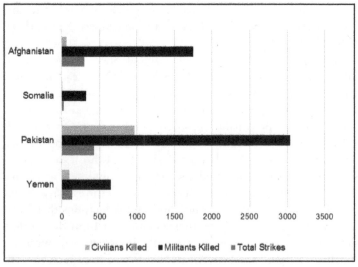

Source: © The Bureau of Investigative Journalism

one. Drone warfare has deeply affected the mentality of both the people who employ it and those it is employed against. In addition, there are doubts as to how effective these platforms are in addressing threats to peace and security. Not least, because of the likelihood of creating further terrorists when the lives of ordinary people are disrupted by the ruthless efficiency with which American industrial counter terrorism is executed in far-off lands. One respected Yemeni journalist, Farea al Muslimi, has described the effects of a drone strike on his village in Yemen. In testimony before the US Senate, he said that few people in the US or Yemen would lose sleep over the targeting of a well-known al-Qaeda operative. However, he questioned the strategic implications this had for relationships between the people of both countries:

> The people in my village wanted Al-Radmi to be captured, so that they could question him and find out what he was doing wrong so they could put an end to it. They still don't have an answer to that question. Instead, all they have is the psychological fear and terror that now occupies their souls. They fear that their home or a neighbor's home could be bombed at any time by a US drone.[139]

It is clear that while these kinds of weapons may decrease the risk to those who operate them, they do very little to win the battle for 'hearts and minds', a vital aspect of any irregular war.

In legal terms, the employment of drones, like ground troops and combat aircraft, in places like Yemen, Pakistan and Afghanistan is an infringement of the sovereignty of that state if consent is not sought or given. In *jus ad bellum* terms, the assassination of key leaders must pass the threshold of presenting an imminent threat to the security of a state. For this to be legal the action must be either in self-defence or authorized by the UN Security Council, but it must also be proportionate. It is difficult to see how the use of drone strikes in certain, recent cases can be justified along these lines. The legality of drone attacks is made yet more dubious when one considers the guiding principles of *jus in bello*. At what point can one distinguish between someone directly participating in hostilities (known as DPH'ing) and a civilian going about his or her normal daily routine? There are no easy answers to these questions and they are likely to come increasingly to the fore as we witness the proliferation of new technologies, weapons systems and platforms for fighting wars.

CYBER WAR

In his confirmation hearing before the US Armed Services Commit-tee on Capitol Hill in 2011, Leon Panetta warned that the 'next Pearl Harbor that we confront could very well be a cyberattack' and might well cripple America's electrical grid and financial systems.[140] The use of the noun 'cyber' as a prefix for new and emerging secu-rity challenges is now commonplace. The development of personal computing and information management systems has seen mili-taries and security agencies come to depend more on technology to safeguard states and their public and private sectors. Professor Thomas Rid has made the audacious case that despite such dismal prospects, cyber war will not take place. 'No cyber offense has ever caused the loss of human life. No cyber offense has ever injured a person,' he argues. 'No cyber attack has ever seriously damaged a building.' In Rid's view, the idea of a 'fifth domain' is a misno-mer and, in fact, cyber offences are 'an attack on violence itself'.[141] Nevertheless, it is difficult to sidestep the reality that new technolo-gies have made it easier to kill and that the advent of new weapons systems has led to some profound changes in tactics.[142]

From the employment of the spear, sword and longbow in battle to the invention of gunpowder and the advent of the cannon, self-loading rifle and tank, weapons have become increasingly important to the business of warfare. The technological transfor-mation in the means and methods of war has led some experts to declare the end of 'old wars' and the advent of 'new wars'. The end of the Cold War brought with it the emergence of some game-changing technological advances as Western states opted to expand their Research and Development programmes in anticipation of a coming Revolution in Military Affairs (RMA). A turn towards RMA prioritized 'shock and awe' tactics from 30,000 feet, over and above infantry- and cavalry-led ground offensives, in which 'surgical strikes' and 'precision-guided' missiles replaced the need for human interaction on the battlefield. As the post-9/11 wars have shown, however, RMA proved short-lived and, instead, there has been a return to the older and more established forms of irregular and regular war.

In this kind of warfare infantry soldiers once again were called upon to interact with local civilian populations, with assistance from a diverse array of sophisticated nano-satellites, UAVs, Intelligence, Surveillance, Target Acquisition and Reconnaissance (ISTAR) assets and advanced force protection equipment. It would seem that the net outcome of all of this technological development has been the reluctant realization that wars in the foreseeable future, like wars in the past, promise to be intensely human affairs, and an increasing drain on financial, as well as human, resources. As was true in previous armed conflicts, this new technology raises profound questions – about who is targeted, and why; about civilian casualties, and the risk of creating new enemies; about the legality of such strikes under US and International Law; and about the accountability and morality of such decisions taken by politicians in capitals far removed from the immediate battleground.

This chapter has suggested that states have not been terribly effective in meeting the 'cognitive challenge of war', and nor have they been clear on how new technologies help to accomplish policy goals such as the defeat of terrorism. With the proliferation of new technology, it is worth asking how far the wisdom of utilizing it has matched the moral and ethical questions thrown up by its application. It could be argued that an air gap has opened up between the employment of new technologies (i.e.

the means) in the targeted killing of suspected terrorists with UAVs on the one hand, and due process of law and the right to a fair trial on the other. It has also led to a backlash in some countries by people who believe they are being unfairly targeted. This is likely to lead to long-term difficulties for governments who wish to win support at home and abroad for the use of such platforms.

Having explored the current state of play in relation to the changing character of war, it seems that terrorists and insurgents have outmanoeuvred modern militaries by their willingness to adapt in the face of superior numbers and firepower. Although the future is by no means certain, it stands to reason that a repeated inability to reconcile ends with means will continue to limit the options open to states and enable their opponents to exploit their vulnerabilities. The unwillingness of Western states to recognize that there is a dark side to their efforts to intervene in so-called failing states means that war in the future is likely to outpace their cognitive ability to understand it.

6

Leaders and followers

In Émile Zola's *La Débâcle* (*The Debacle*) the decline and fall of Napoleon III's Second Empire form the backdrop to the pitiful and ruinous battles of the Franco-Prussian War of 1870–1. French troops put up an unimpressive fight against the more technologically sophisticated and better-equipped Germans, which ended in defeat on the field of battle and Napoleon's surrender seven weeks later to the Prussian king, William I, who would subsequently become emperor (or kaiser) after the unification of Germany in 1871. Zola's story paints a dreary and pitiful picture of how the men of the 106th Regiment – many eager and willing to fight, despite being poorly fed and led – come to resent soldiering. Once despondency takes root, their morale suffers irreparable damage and primary group cohesion, recognized by sociologists as essential for fighting, breaks down. The results become obvious a third of the way into the novel:

> Now they dragged their feet in angry silence, hating their rifles which bruised their shoulders and the packs that weighed them down, having lost all faith in their commanders and giving way to such hopelessness that they were only marching ahead like a herd of cattle lashed by the whip of fate. The wretched army was beginning to climb its hill of Calvary.[143]

There can be no question that, had they been better fed, equipped, trained and led, the French would have enjoyed at least a modicum of success in this brief war. Ironically, the underperformance of the soldiers and their officers sits in marked contrast to the actions of the French army at Waterloo in 1815.

As one of the world's best-known battles, Waterloo saw two of the era's greatest military commanders, Napoleon Bonaparte and the Duke of Wellington, fight it out on a battlefield that, incredibly, measured only 2.5 miles by 2.5 miles. The congested nature of the fighting and the immediacy of the killing typified war in the nineteenth century, where battles were smothered by the smoke and noise from the muskets and cannon fire of two opposing, uniformed armies. When the smoke cleared, it exposed the screams of injured men and came to be seen by those who survived it as a 'slaughter house'. In the first ten hours of the Battle of Waterloo some 40,000 soldiers and several thousand horses were killed or wounded. What kept the men fighting in the eyes of many of its veterans was the presence of the two leaders throughout the battle. These leaders made swift decisions, they led from the front, and they knew intimately how to control those who followed them, said the veterans. But was that really what made the difference at Waterloo or the countless other battles they fought? And, moreover, what contribution do the people that follow leaders in war actually make to the outcome?

Historian Eric Hobsbawm was not altogether convinced that Napoleon's brilliance as a leader could be reduced to showing his face amidst the bloody fighting of battles like Waterloo. He believed there was more to it than that:

> The extraordinary power of this myth can be adequately explained neither by Napoleonic victories nor by Napoleonic propaganda, nor even by Napoleon's own undoubted genius. As a man he was unquestionably very brilliant, versatile, intelligent and imaginative, though power

made him rather nasty. As a general he had no equal; as a ruler he was a superbly efficient planner, chief and executive and sufficient of an all-round intellectual to understand and supervise what his subordinates were doing.[144]

For Hobsbawm, Napoleon proved effective not only because he led from the front but because he could manage his troops well, and they, in turn, believed in what they were doing. In other words, they had invested in the task to which he had committed them. That was not all. Napoleon also understood the context in which his decisions played out. He knew he had limitations and, therefore, had to rely upon both coercion (the stick) and consent (the carrot) to ensure he could achieve his objectives.

To understand the development of leadership, we need to go back before Napoleon's time to that of Alexander the Great, the Greek general and conqueror who reigned as King of Macedon between 336 and 323 BCE. One of Napoleon's great heroes, Alexander won most of his greatest victories before his thirty-sixth birthday. But how did he do that? 'What we do know, and can be absolutely certain of', argues historian Paul Cartledge, 'is that there was something about Alexander that inspired extraordinary personal devotion. He gave his soldiers the sense that, with him, nothing was impossible.'[145] From this vantage point we can see that Alexander inspired the men under his command to the extent that they believed they could do anything he asked of them. In this sense, Alexander drew on deep-rooted consent in order to lead those who followed him. He did this by ensuring the maintenance of morale amongst his troops. At the height of his military prowess in 324 BCE, Alexander commanded some 18,000 troops. Many of these men followed him because he had a proven track record of success. It is perhaps unsurprising that by leading his men to glory on so many occasions, the memory of his greatest exploits was kept alive by those who followed him. So, in this sense, the case could be made that it was not necessarily his greatness as a leader that ensured Alexander's military exploits passed into history, but rather the bond he shared with those who followed him, a bond largely based on success and consent.

One hundred years after the Battle of Waterloo the idea of a leader sticking close to the action had become an anachronism just as surely as the cavalry charge against tanks at the outbreak of the Second World War. In the First World War, leaders depended much more on coercion and the creation and sustainment of a 'greater cause' to inspire men in battles, especially in those countries where liberal democracy formed the cornerstone of the state. From the time of Clausewitz, it has been essential for generals and politicians to appreciate the nature of the war they are prosecuting, lest they risk defeat and ruin. Leaders, therefore, need a good appreciation not only of what makes their followers tick but also how this relates to the context of the war they are fighting. In order to assess the importance of these factors – leadership strategies, the relationship of leaders to followers, and the context in which they operate – it is useful to turn to some illustrative examples.

Leaders

It is often said that at its most basic, leadership is about getting people to do what they wouldn't normally do. This could be charging an enemy position all guns blazing or risking life and limb to rescue a wounded comrade under fire. In his conquest of Ireland on behalf of the English Parliament in 1649–50, Oliver Cromwell made important and long-lasting strategic decisions based on his appreciation of the contextual factors beyond those just concerning the military. A professional politician cum amateur military commander, Cromwell would nevertheless come to earn a reputation for ruthlessness in battle. Having invested a sizeable amount of his own money in the reconquest of Ireland (to help pay and equip his men), he launched a war of sieges to retake those Irish towns that had rebelled against English rule. Offering what he considered to be generous terms, those who accepted were spared; those who did not were massacred, most infamously at Drogheda in 1649, or enslaved and sent overseas to penal colonies in the Caribbean islands. Historians generally agree that Cromwell employed brutal and – in some cases – inhumane tactics in suppressing the Irish.

We now know that Cromwell turned his attention to Ireland in the first place for two principal reasons – one external and one internal. On the one hand, Charles Stuart, son of the executed king, had landed in Jersey on his way to Ireland, thus raising the prospect of a foreign-backed invasion of England. On the other hand, the economic situation in England was such that the financial burden could no longer be borne by the English alone. The neighbouring island of Ireland was seen in many ways as England's first colony, and Cromwell believed he could exploit it to help ease the taxation burden on Parliamentary supporters at home. Land would be seized and redistributed as 'spoils of war', with Cromwell guaranteed some land in Offaly in exchange for his heavy personal investment in the campaign. Ruthless though it was, Cromwell's campaign fulfilled wider strategic objectives he had helped to set. An added dimension to his success throughout the entire revolutionary period was his establishment of a regular standing army in England that responded to a clear chain of command. By the time he became Lord Protector in 1653, Cromwell had successfully combined the roles of military and political leader.

It was Irish playwright George Bernard Shaw who once observed that 'We speak of war gods, but not of mathematician gods, poet or painter gods, or inventor gods.' In what he regarded as a 'primitive blood sport that gratifies human pugnacity', Shaw clearly felt little compunction for those he considered warmongers.

We worship all the conquerors but have only one Prince of Peace, who was horribly put to death, and, if he lived today in these islands, would have some difficulty in getting exempt from military service as a conscientious objector, if indeed he did not catch the war infection and head the rush to enlist.[146]

The image of a wartime leader as a godless warmonger, intoxicated by patriotism, is a powerfully seductive one. However, it neglects the fact that leadership is a practical activity that is increasingly thought of as a two-way street where leaders depend on the compliance of followers to enable them to lead. The critique of the all-powerful leaders also neglects the relationship between leaders and followers and the context which gives their actions meaning.[147] The role of leaders, in war or in peace, is, of course, critical. Leadership expert Keith Grint informs us that leaders are 'limited and dependent upon the actions of subordinates, and indeed their own preparation for the "big" decision that may derive from the accumulation of many small acts and decisions'.[148]

The idea of a leader making 'the big' decision and, thereby, automatically commanding the respect and affection of his men has a long lineage. The Roman general (and later emperor) Julius Caesar is said to have been the adhesive around which his empire's might coalesced. Everyone, civilian and military, looked to Caesar for direction. In reality, he was indebted to, amongst other things, the collective obedience of the Roman Legion, easily the best collective fighting machine the world had ever seen until that point. What made the Legion so formidable was the scope given to individual initiative. The Legion was to be feared not only for the momentum of its mass, but because of the courage and ferocity of its individual soldiers. Many of them were veterans, who had seen bloody fighting first-hand, and Caesar depended on this expertise to accomplish missions that were sometimes very complex affairs. To aid him, the legionary had the most advanced weaponry of the times and became skilled in intricate military strategies, like siege warfare, that would test brains as well as brawn. The affection, respect and confidence Romans held for Caesar ensured that they were sufficiently motivated to accomplish these difficult and demanding tasks in war.

Leaders like Caesar were great because they could encourage greatness in their subordinates. One of the twenty-first century's most proficient advocates of network-centric (rather than leader-centric) leadership is General Stanley McChrystal. He has propounded the view that leadership has an important facilitating function in modern war:

> Leadership is neither good nor evil. We like to equate leaders with values we admire, but the two can be separate and distinct. Self-serving or evil intent motivated some of the most effective leaders I saw, like Abu Musab al-Zarqawi. In the end, leadership is a skill that can be used like any other, but with far greater effect.[149]

For McChrystal, leadership is a catalyst for organizing and driving forward men and women in battle, often in the face of great hardships and privations. He recognized that leaders frequently have to bully, cajole or inspire their followers in order to attain an objective. However, McChrystal believed that leadership was more about the empowerment of the team, rather than simply the individual leader or follower.

The need to preserve team cohesion in war presents its own unique challenges and is often dependent on the character of the war being fought. Those pursuing an irregular form of warfare can sometimes face insurmountable odds that they might think impossible. In this case, it is vital for leaders to recognize the challenges and to assist their team in overcoming them. Take the example of Brendan Hughes, a well-respected officer in the Provisional Irish Republican Army (Provisional IRA), a paramilitary organization fighting to obtain a united Ireland, free of British influence, in the late twentieth century. Regarded as a guerrilla leader with 'a common touch', Hughes's leadership qualities were noted both by his comrades and by his enemies in the British Army and the Royal Ulster Constabulary.[150] By 1969, the re-emergence of intercommunal strife between Catholic nationalists and Protestant unionists had grown in severity, thereby necessitating the deployment of British soldiers onto the streets to keep the two sides apart. Within the space of eighteen months, relations between the Catholic community and the troops had deteriorated to such an extent that the Provisional IRA was able to claim that it was needed to defend the Catholic community against Protestant attacks. The army and police found themselves increasingly drawn into the violence and, following a decision by the Provisional IRA to take the war to the 'old enemy', republicans began an armed campaign that would last for thirty years and cause almost 4,000 deaths and ten times as many injuries.

As a key Provisional IRA figure in Belfast, Brendan Hughes was responsible for planning and executing the organization's military operations, which included bombings, shootings and counter-intelligence. To those volunteers who served under him, he was regarded as a risk-taker who preferred to endure the same hardships as those he sent out to kill. As one of his subordinates later wrote of him, 'Brendan Hughes sought no personal gain. He was a giant of a man, a Republican leader who led from the front. He asked no volunteer to do what he would not do himself; he fought side by side with his volunteers.'[151] In his role as a leader, Hughes demonstrated an ability to work collaboratively with his subordinates to achieve the overarching objectives of his organization.

Leaders who think of themselves as a 'soldier's soldier' are rare because most military organizations tend to forego egalitarianism for a clear distinction between officers and other ranks. They are also rare because they tend to act out of a greater adherence to elitist values. In the closing stages of the Pacific War, General Tadamichi Kuribayashi had been given the task of defending the strategically important island of Iwo Jima. A family man with three young children, he lived his life frugally, despite being a member of the landed gentry. Consequently, he took the decision to live with the same dangers as his men. He had a very simple plan to draw US forces inland and then to ambush them by throwing everything he had at them. Thirty-six days into a battle that was supposed to last only five, Kuribayashi led a death charge of his last remaining 900 men, with the remaining wounded blowing themselves up with their hand grenades. Sixty thousand Marines had landed in Iwo Jima and incurred 28,686 casualties, almost 7,000 fatal. General Kuribayashi sacrificed himself for the same reasons that pervaded the thinking of his brother officer, General Yamashita; he could not return home with defeat on his conscience and so that left little option other than to seek victory or death. Soldiers followed their general in this instance because they shared similar values from a culture that prided itself on victory at all costs.

GENERAL DAVID PETRAEUS'S SPEECH AT SANDHURST ON LEADERSHIP (2011)

First, lead by example. Your soldiers will look to you for information and will follow your lead. Think carefully about that. Everything you do will be scrutinized, emulated, and commented on by those you're privileged to lead. If you lean forward and drive on with your mission, those in your charge will too. If you make light of adversity, your soldiers will follow suit. But if you ease off, if you let down, they will do the same.

Second, listen and learn. Recognize that those you will lead – and, in particular, your noncommissioned officers – will have a lot to teach you. Indeed, many of your soldiers will have already experienced near-continuous combat going back several years. Listening to them – and heeding their advice – will pay dividends.

Third, make decisions. When the listening is done and the time for decision is at hand, you must make the call. There will be many of those moments when all eyes turn to you for a decision. Be ready for them. They will matter.

Fourth, lead from the front. In virtually every activity – with the possible exception of going through the mess hall – you need to be visible and lead the way. That means you must have the physical ability, the technical competence, and the personal attributes needed to inspire those who will follow. Never forget that it's hard to lead from the rear of the formation.

Fifth, keep your soldiers informed. Each of your troops can be the most important soldier at a given point on a given battlefield on a given day. Each must thus know not only how, but why. If you take care of your soldiers and explain the importance of what they're doing, they'll follow your lead and embrace the mission.

Sixth, lead and build your team. Keep in mind that, as a leader, it's all about the team. Before you came to Sandhurst, you were probably graded on your personal performance. As a military leader, however, you'll be graded on how your unit does. Remember that there is no such thing as a squared-away platoon leader with a screwed-up platoon.

As the story of Iwo Jima illustrates, some of the most exemplary leadership displayed in combat has come from those who have found themselves at a disadvantage, where the overriding commitment to a shared goal has carried the day. In the Cuban revolutionary war of the 1950s, Fidel Castro emerged as a charismatic man of action, capable of mobilizing ordinary people – students, workers and peasants – to follow him in his mission to overthrow the Batista military regime in Havana. Castro was lucky in that he could also rely on the inspirational leadership provided by two of his right-hand *compañeros*, his brother Raul Castro and his comrade in arms Ernesto 'Che' Guevara. Che, an Argentinian-born physician, became one of the legendary leaders of the columns Castro fielded to engage Batista's troops in combat. As his biographer wrote of him:

> Guevara's enormous contribution to the struggle, his bravery, discipline, organization, and levelheadedness. The very traits that at first the Cubans tended to dislike eventually made him indispensable. His Argentine and European sense of order, his punctuality and formality, his respect for the rules, his insistence on honoring promises and commitments, were not Caribbean virtues by any means. Indeed, it was their rarity which made them so precious during the final phase of the war.[152]

Che inspired his men, led them boldly through the jungle and fought alongside them in ferocious gun battles with superior forces. Although he had faults – he was by no means a perfect leader and would often shout abuse at his subordinates and coerce them into battle – he was revered by those who followed him. 'He was exemplary. He had great moral authority over his troops, great leadership,' Castro later said of him. 'I believe he was a model for the revolutionary man.'[153] As with so many other leaders, Che Guevara understood his own limitations and those of his subordinates, though his understanding of the political context of their actions would eventually lead them to victory.

Followers

It is generally accepted that leadership is different from command, for the former relies on consent and attractiveness more than the latter, which relies disproportionately on coercion and a clear hierarchy. In military organizations, which are often structured hierarchically, success depends on everyone knowing and accepting their place. For this to work, it must be based on the humility of both the leader and the follower. If they are task-orientated, as the preceding discussion on leadership has indicated that they need to be, then effective leaders will engender in those below them a sense of ownership over the task or mission. But is it true to say that followers are always motivated by shared chivalrous values of patriotism, ideology or politics, or are they simply following a leader because they have been inspired to do great things, regardless of the opposition they are likely to face in war? With that in mind, is it actually the case that great leaders are great facilitators, and that what they and followers achieve together as a team is the most important part of the relationship?

Before we address these questions in detail, it is worth considering the reasons why people joined military organizations when they first became instruments of states several hundred years ago. In the eighteenth century, we know that some men were simply press-ganged or tricked into military service, but most were not and enlisted voluntarily. Of these, writes military historian Christopher Duffy, a sizeable number did so because of an 'inability to manage their affairs'. In Poland, southern Germany, France and Italy, recruits to the Prussian army included 'noblemen, runaway monks, doctors, lecturers and many other learned men, as well as merchants, apothecaries, former officials, craftsmen, artists, actors and jugglers',[154] all of whom ended up as private soldiers. Despite attracting skilled workers and professionals, armies were not complete without those from more dubious and unfortunate backgrounds. It was the French Minister of War, Claude Louis, Comte de Saint-Germain, who coined the most infamous remark about those enlisting from the lower orders. 'Armies must inevitably be composed of the filth of the nation, and everything which is useless and harmful to society,' he said. 'We must refer to military discipline as the means of purifying this corrupt mass, of shaping it and making it useful.'[155] In armies like these, where coercion and fear ruled supreme, leaders tended to run the very real risk of catching a stray bullet fired by their own men, a historical antecedent of what became known as 'fragging' in the Vietnam War.

One of Britain's most experienced generals of the postwar period, Hughie Stockwell, believed strongly in the role of discipline as a form of coercively enforcing standards on ordinary fighting men. Recounting his time on military operations in Palestine in the late 1940s, Stockwell wrote:

> Every officer and soldier by his personal behaviour, turnout, smartness, soldierly bearing and alertness, is the very best of advertisement to the security force and the soundest way of 'showing the flag'. Ill-discipline, bad turnout, slovenliness, drunkenness, thefts, 'beat-ups', lack of courtesy and good manners generally, by officers and men of the security forces, do as much to lower morale and lessen the faith of the civil population and play into the hands of the 'thug', as does any lack of a strong policy by a weak government.[156]

In the British case, social class has played a key role in ensuring the chain of command is respected. This has been captured in one of the best-known novels about the Second World War, *The Bridge over the River Kwai* by Pierre Boulle, which features a stiff-upper-lip officer in the form of Lieutenant Colonel Nicholson. He is a man for whom honour, even when living amidst one's enemies, is necessary, even vital, to the continuation of civilization itself in the face of the 'savages' as represented by the Japanese soldiers.

Nicholson appears to be representative of the culture commonly found in British society at that time. The leader is a man not only distant from his subordinates in terms of military rank but also, crucially, in terms of social rank. It is expressed by Boulle's depiction of the back-breaking work keeping ordinary soldiers busy while interned in horrendous conditions in a

Japanese prisoner-of-war camp. Nicholson, by contrast, is spared menial work by the fact that he is an officer. The British soldier, we discover in the book, is hard-working and confident in his chain of command. In the River Kwai camp, they have a high opinion of Colonel Nicholson for the stiff-upper-lip resistance that carries him through his dealing with the Japanese.[157]

The class system in Britain extended well beyond the Second World War and would affect the way Britain fought its wars of decolonization, in places such as Malaya and Kenya, in the 1950s. The average squaddie was expected to take to killing as if it were an extension of his natural proletarian role in civilian life, whether that was performed in a coal mine, on a factory assembly line or at sea on board a merchant vessel. In war, as in peace, the British soldier would be subject to the division of labour (filling every minute of his time with 'hard work, and cheerfulness and health', according to Boulle), while his officer would be free to 'command' from the harsh reality of 'light duties'. If we probe Boulle's novel further, we discover that Colonel Nicholson's 'resistance' actually has more to do with maintaining the English class system than it has with challenging Japanese fascist rule. And when his soldiers do revolt, it appears that this was merely a protest against 'an attitude and code of behaviour which clashed with their instinctive urge to do a job properly'.[158]

The unquestioning obedience of British soldiers to the chain of command – backed up by a deeply embedded class system – has not always been reflected in other imperial armies. Zola's depiction of the Franco-Prussian War shows that the individual gripes of ordinary soldiers, if left unchecked, can seriously undermine the cohesion of armies in war. In *La Débâcle*, one of the characters, a bar-stool revolutionary and all-round Parisian smart alec, declares: 'And what about these famous victories? And that was a nice joke too, when they told us Bismarck had been taken prisoner and that they had kicked a whole army of them into a quarry ... Balls! They are fucking well having us on!'[159] The despondency that sometimes accompanies the monotony of military service has been reflected by others in more recent times. 'Three-quarters of military discipline is mindless, obsolete and wastefully self-frustrating – apart, of course, from being highly irritating,' one former soldier told military historian Richard Holmes. 'No one can serve in any army for years without being to some extent an inbred malingerer and scrounger, irredeemably slothful.'[160]

There can be little doubt that military culture like this is about reinforcing obedience, often by way of coercion. Having had his own brush with enlistment in the ranks of the British Army during the Second World War, Eric Hobsbawm looked negatively upon military service as 'a means of securing the loyalty … of citizens with troubling sympathies for mass movements which undermined the social and political order'.[161] It is not without reason, therefore, that states have sought to create a collective bond between their troops in a way that privileges loyalty and obedience above all other traits.

The enforcement of obedience might well have worked in the British Army during the Second World War because of the added class dimension, but it did not hold in other armies. Liberal intellectual Gore Vidal, the doyen of American foreign policy critics, noted how US soldiers were not well motivated when it came to the Vietnam War:

> It should be noted that the American fighting man has been pretty lousy from the beginning of the republic, and more power to him. He has no desire to kill strangers or get hurt himself. He does not like to be told what to do. For him, there is neither duty nor honor; his country is his skin. This does not make for a world conqueror.[162]

The reluctance on the part of the American soldier to bend so readily to obedience lies in stark contrast to the attitude of Japanese *Tokkō Tai* pilots (known as kamikazes outside Japan), tasked with flying suicide missions in the Pacific campaign of the Second World War, and in whom we see a tremendous commitment to serving the state even to the extent of sacrificing one's own life deliberately. Curiously, those selected for such deadly operations were often young students educated to a high standard. They were widely read – having consulted everything from Immanuel Kant and Karl Marx to Oscar Wilde and Gustav Flaubert – and found solace and purpose in the inspiration of the classic philosophers, especially those who advocated sacrifice of the individual for the good of mankind.

Although the Japanese kamikazes demonstrated considerable self-control and unswerving commitment to their chain of command, this has not always been reflected in other places and times in which powerful ideologies hold sway and are thought to animate those whom they send off to do battle with the enemy. In one of the most significant novels ever published on the Vietnam War, Bao Ninh's *The Sorrow of War*, we find a protagonist in the shape of Kien unsure whether he is really fighting for his country or because he is ordered to do so by a central Communist elite only interested in their narrow party objectives. Kien's unit, Battalion 27, was wiped out in a bloody and decisive battle with US troops in the Central Highlands in 1973 and the story follows our protagonist as he returns a year later to collect the remains of his comrades.

The Sorrow of War centres on this young man's struggle to come to terms with what he has seen in the war. As one of only ten survivors from a battalion of over 500, he recalls bodies having been incinerated in their tanks or obliterated where they sheltered from the bombardment. The dropping of napalm by American war planes mixed with blood-curdling screams haunts Kien's narrative. It is a story of how human beings turn to each other, to religion, and to a variety of other coping mechanisms to get through the day, when the only certainty in their lives is death. In this, he believes he shares 'the fate of an insect or an ant in the war'.[163] Kien is terrified by one of his fellow soldiers unloading his problems on him and thinks he would rather throw himself off a waterfall than listen to the whinging of others. This is a war whose victims are young men. In a conversation with a boy soldier named Can, it becomes clear that the young man wishes to desert. 'I haven't lived yet and I want very much to live.' In *The Sorrow of War* we hear of North Vietnamese troops deserting 'as though soldiers were being vomited out, emptying the insides of whole platoons'.[164]

ENFORCING COMPLIANCE – AN EXTRACT FROM THE IRA'S *GREEN BOOK*

The Provisional IRA was one of the twentieth century's most sophisticated terrorist organizations. It enforced a harsh regime of discipline on its members in a conflict that saw the organization take the lives of almost 2,000 people, including British security forces, its own members and those of rival paramilitary groups, as well as Protestant and Catholic civilians, in an armed campaign that lasted from 1970 until 2005. This is an extract from its membership code of conduct:

Volunteers are expected to wage a military war of liberation against a numerically superior force. This involves the use of arms and explosives. Firstly the use of arms. When volunteers are trained in the use of arms they must fully understand that guns are dangerous, and their main purpose is to take human life, in other words to kill people, and volunteers are trained to kill people. It is not an easy thing to take up a gun and go out to kill some person without strong convictions or justification. The Army, its motivating force, is based upon strong convictions which bonds the Army into one force and before any potential volunteer decides to join the Army he must have these strong convictions. Convictions which are strong enough to give him confidence to kill someone without hesitation and without regret. Again all people wishing to join the Army must fully realize that when life is being taken, that very well could mean their own. If you go out to shoot soldiers or police you must fully realize that they too can shoot you. Life in an underground army is extremely harsh and hard, cruel and disillusioning at times. So before any person decides to join the Army he should think seriously about the whole thing.[165]

The coercive structure of autocratic military organizations, like the North Vietnamese Army in the 1970s, means leaders must inspire troops to do things they would not otherwise do and, when that fails, they must make examples of those they deem weak or cowardly. In the case of Can, his skeleton is later discovered by military policemen. 'That damned turncoat, he really stank', recalls the policeman who buried him where he fell. There is much resentment in Ninh's book about how ordinary peasants – the bulk of those who did the fighting – had no real say in how the war turned out. By highlighting the pathetic nature of the killing and dying, *The Sorrow of War* ranks alongside George Orwell's *Homage to Catalonia* for its challenging of assumptions about why people fight in wars and how they come to terms with this when they leave the war behind. While it is perhaps more common for war stories to grow in the telling, both of these books depict the reality of war from the point of view of followers rather than leaders. Respected war correspondent Anthony Lloyd has written movingly and honestly about his experiences of why people become involved in war. 'All participants lie in war,' he assures us, when considering their reasons for fighting: 'It is natural. Some often, some all the time: UN spokesmen, Croats, Serbs, Muslims, the lot. Truth is a weapon more than a casualty. Used to persuade people of one thing or another, it becomes propaganda. The more authoritative the figure, the bigger the lies; the more credible his position, the better the lies.'[166] And it is Lloyd's recommendation that if one wishes to see the reality of war, it is best not to start looking at the chain of command. 'Why waste time listening to an officer in a headquarters crank out the party line', he asks, 'when you could see the reality of a situation for yourself in the dirty bunkers up the way?'[167]

The masking of truth when it comes to war is a way of maintaining morale. Focusing on a higher political purpose remains an important – if often inadequate – adhesive for binding together those soldiers who become disillusioned with the intimacy of fighting and dying. Russian involvement in Chechnya cost the lives of 15,000 soldiers, with three times as many wounded. Conscripts were frequently sent straight to the front line and returned in coffins. One mother's story reflects the anguish families frequently undergo when their loved ones are deployed into a war:

> She cried when Nikolai was drafted into the army. She'd heard about boys who had been sent straight to Chechnya after basic training and who'd come home in zinc coffins. Or maimed. Or with grenade shock. Some returned home like different people. They lashed out, screamed, drank. Like the neighbour across the hall. He had gone mad in Afghanistan. Since he'd come home in 1989, all hell had broken loose, every night.[168]

From this extract, it would be easy to see soldiers as victims caught up by the calamity of war. Yet this is much too simplistic. Some unquestionably do experience doubts about their wartime service and, at times, this has spilt over into quiet indignation for those who led them into the war in the first place. Yet there are many soldiers around the world who remain quietly proud of their military service and make an annual pilgrimage each year to commemorate the sacrifice of comrades who did not come home from war.

Although much of what we know about leaders and their followers comes from the act of fighting in wars, we must also accept that much of this service is distinguished more by large periods of inactivity with only occasional bouts of excitement. In Joseph Heller's satire *Catch-22*, his protagonist Yossarian struggles with the concept of flying missions to bomb targets. When his friend Nate is killed in a bomb run, Yossarian refuses to fight. Two colonels discuss his refusal. He is spared a court martial for failing to carry out a lawful order because of his courage in the face of enemy fire. Like so many other cases noted above, it is not only the coercive military system that keeps Yossarian at war, but his commanding officer and other leaders. Despite his rebelliousness, Yossarian's plight exposes the black-and-white nature of the relationship between leaders and followers. In the case of leaders, they might be much more fixated on the bigger picture in war – on concepts of 'win' or 'lose' – but their followers will have a much simpler view of what is going on and concentrate their attention more on personal survival than higher political goals.

It is common to decry war as a deeply asocial or antisocial phenomenon. The dislocation it causes in human relationships, the destruction to the environment in which it is fought, and the far-reaching consequences it has for the political, social and economic aspects of life after war are obvious. This chapter has examined the human aspects of leadership and the sorts of traits that are common to those who come to be regarded as 'war gods'. It has also explained that for a leader to become a leader he or she must have followers. In recent years, research into followership has suggested that it is just as important as leadership in ensuring success, whether in war or in peace. It also tells us that we must look to the context in which this relationship emerges so as to understand its dynamics fully. The next chapter considers the importance of this human dimension of war when it comes to ending fighting and building a sustainable peace. Once again we will see that context really matters.

7

Ending wars

It was a beautiful sunny morning on 6 August 1945. At 8.15 A.M., Taeko Teramae, a teenager working in the Central Telephone Bureau, was on a break in a restroom when she glanced out of the window to see 'something shining falling down', which grew larger and larger as it reached the ground. 'And just when I was thinking about what it was, it blasted with a flash. The flash was so strong that I thought my body would be melted,' she later recalled.[169] Her friends who were outside on the roof being briefed about their day's duties were incinerated by the atomic bomb that had just been dropped on the city.

Some 80,000 men, women and children perished immediately when the United States dropped a 9,000-pound uranium bomb (known as 'Little Boy') on the Japanese city of Hiroshima. Hundreds of thousands more were directly affected by the nuclear blast, which obliterated approximately ninety percent of the city. Three days later the US dropped a heavier, 10,000-pound plutonium bomb (known as 'Fat Man') on Nagasaki, killing at least 50,000 people. These attacks are the only time nuclear weapons have been used during wartime. The suffering of Japanese civilians amidst the ruins of these cities provides a powerful testament to the human consequences of war, especially when states are prepared to use WMDs as a means of securing their political objectives.

The then US president, Harry S. Truman, justified his administration's actions by citing the failure of the Japanese High Command to surrender in the wake of an ultimatum issued at Potsdam on 26 July 1945. 'We spent two billion dollars on the greatest scientific gamble in history – and won,' Truman said in a press release. 'If they do not now accept our terms they may expect a rain of ruin from the air, the like of which has never been seen on this earth.' Truman believed that atomic power could 'become a powerful and forceful influence towards the maintenance of world peace'.[170] And it would seem to be the case. The unconditional surrender of the Japanese on 15 August 1945 suggests that the employment of nuclear weapons at this point in the Second World War hastened the end of the war.

There have been challenges to this view, however. Professor Ward Wilson has undertaken an extensive analysis of the Japanese, Russian and United States sources and concludes that Tokyo surrendered not because of the bombing of Nagasaki, or even Hiroshima, but because of the Soviet declaration of war on Japan on 8 August 1945.[171] This interpretation of the impact of nuclear weapons in the Pacific War suggests that actually the conventional

---

EXTRACT FROM THE JAPANESE INSTRUMENT OF SURRENDER, 2 SEPTEMBER 1945

We, acting by command of and on behalf of the Emperor of Japan, the Japanese Government and the Japanese Imperial General Headquarters, hereby accept the provisions set forth in the declaration issued by the heads of the Governments of the United States, China and Great Britain on 26 July 1945, at Potsdam, and subsequently adhered to by the Union of Soviet Socialist Republics, which four powers are hereafter referred to as the Allied Powers.

We hereby proclaim the unconditional surrender to the Allied Powers of the Japanese Imperial General Headquarters and of all Japanese armed forces and all armed forces under Japanese control wherever situated.[172]

bombing of sixty-eight Japanese cities throughout the summer of 1945 had more of a decisive impact on strategic thinking in Tokyo than the August attacks. If we accept that there is indeed some truth to these claims, it follows that it is perhaps more unusual for wars to end with such finality or permanence. So, the question asked in this chapter is: what makes wars eventually end?

How wars end

'Only the dead are safe; only the dead have seen the end of war' runs the well-worn adage coined by Spanish philosopher George Santayana. What is often missed is the second half of Santayana's aphorism, which reads: 'Not that non-existence deserves to be called peace; it is only by an illusion of contrast and a pathetic fallacy that we are tempted to call it so.'[173] This is perhaps one of the most profound meditations on war ever written. Much earlier than Santayana, the Athenian chronicler of war Thucydides expressed a similar scepticism about peace. In the classical period, peace and war were driven by the same factors of self-interest, chance and passion. We can see this quite clearly when we look at the peace treaty and alliance agreed by Sparta and Athens after a devastating ten-year war (431–421 BCE). While some people accepted the accord, others attempted to undermine it. Unsurprisingly, the peace treaty eventually unravelled and the two sides returned to war in order to resolve their differences in a more decisive way.

Earlier chapters have suggested that wars begin for as many different reasons as they are ended. This is by no means an original observation. Most military strategists looking at the philosophical and practical realities of war would argue that although it is necessary to fight, it is only necessary to prolong the fight in order to accomplish the objectives set out by the warring parties. However abhorrent a proposition this might seem to those who see peace as the natural order of things, it is important to recognize that in times of fear and insecurity, war is still the favoured option for those who seek to prosecute it. It is worth reminding ourselves that all wars ought to be fought for the rational purpose of obtaining a 'better state of peace', in Basil Liddell Hart's phrase, but with the important caveat: 'even if only from your own point of view'.[174] As stated in chapter 1, war is the means by which the goal of attaining a political object can be reached – the 'original motive for the war', according to Clausewitz – which 'will thus determine both the military objective and the amount of effort it requires'.[175]

There is a belief amongst experts that decisive victory is more the exception than the rule and that only dialogue can ensure a more sustainable end to war. But is this actually the case? It is certainly true that the failure to secure outright victory is all too evident in regular wars. Famous engagements like the Battle of the Boyne, fought between King William of Orange and King James II in 1690, failed to produce a crushing defeat of the Jacobites and led to some hard questions being asked about how a more durable peace settlement might be achieved since victory appeared so elusive. This has, of course, been the case in more recent irregular wars too. The US-led NATO coalition in Afghanistan between 2001 and 2014 failed to administer a knock-out blow to the Taliban, which made it much harder for the government of Afghanistan to do so after the end of NATO combat operations. Very often, therefore, victory exists in direct contrast to defeat (like in the unconditional surrender of Germany and Japan in 1945), or in the declaration of a truce or ceasefire (as in the case of the first Arab–Israeli War of 1948–9, the Korean War of 1950–3 and the brief war between Russia and Georgia in 1993).

There are certainly other contemporary examples where seeking victory in deeply divided societies can actually prolong conflicts. This usually happens when rival ethnic groups fail to agree not only on the causes of the war but also on how best to prevent its reoccurrence in the future. One has only to look at the instability of the Israeli–Palestinian dispute to see the consequences of the inability, and yet the insistence, of either side to secure a more decisive victory. Despite these obvious failures, signatures on a peace treaty remain a powerfully seductive answer to the question of how we end wars.

On the other hand, there are clear cases where peace treaties fail to bring about peace. In South Asia, for example, experts observing cases of ethnic conflict have arrived at the tentative conclusion that 'the search for a negotiated settlement is not an integral part of war-ending strategies in all cases.'[176] The reason why negotiations typically fail is that when one opponent sues for peace this creates a shift in the power relations between the sides and can expose the weaker opponent to challenges and divisions from within its own state. This happened in Germany in the aftermath of the First World War, in the fledgling Irish Free State after the Anglo-Irish War of Independence concluded with a treaty in 1921, and, of course, in the Fatah–Hamas divide in Palestine after the peace process of the 1990s.

Another way of looking at the issue of why fighting reoccurs is to examine the causes of wars in the early twenty-first century. The head of the NGO International Alert, Dan Smith, makes the convincing case that the international political landscape remains 'disfigured by wars that resume after not only the signing of ceasefires, but even after the conclusion of peace agreements'. In a litany of failed peace agreements from Angola, Burundi, Cambodia, Chechnya and Georgia – a list to which we might add the DRC, Sudan and Nigeria – the tendency to opt for a quick fix has led to greater problems further along the line. This can be easily deduced by taking a quick glance at wars in the 1990s. For example, sixty-six percent of all wars between 1990 and 1999 were more than five years old, while thirty percent had been ongoing for more than twenty years.[177] The reason for the reoccurrence of civil war has been attributed to the fact that, in ninety percent of cases, violence is more likely to reoccur where there has previously been a conflict. Four decades earlier the figure was less than fifty percent.[178] For the vast majority of wars (seventy percent, according to some estimates) it is more likely that they will be 'concluded through negotiation or petering out rather than outright victory or defeat'.[179] This can be seen with the Spanish–American War (1898), in which hostilities between the two sides were suspended by the protocol of 12 August 1898, even though the state of war continued to exist until the US Congress ratified the peace treaty in April 1899.[180] In order to understand the complex reasons why wars end, one must, therefore, examine how and why fighting contributes to the outcome.

Negotiating an end to war

As we noted above, dialogue is believed to be a powerful tool when it comes to ending wars. The evidence suggests talking, rather than killing, is one of the most effective ways of resolving differences amongst human beings. For example, negotiation played an important role in ending some of the worst ethnic conflicts of the twentieth century, such as the Northern Ireland 'troubles' and the fall of apartheid in South Africa. In both of these conflicts, prominent political leaders, like John Hume, David Trimble, F.W. de Klerk and Nelson Mandela, believed that people had been locked in fighting and violence for so long that it was necessary to find a peaceful way out. They opted for compromise rather than continued bloodshed in a way that emphasized the 'win–win' dimension of the prospective peace, rather than the traditional 'win–lose' outcome common in wars.

The emergence of the UN in the immediate aftermath of the Second World War demonstrated that human beings could cooperate for the greater good. In tune with earlier treaties, such as the Kellogg–Briand Pact of 1928, the UN Charter (1945) was drafted to ensure that war, especially between states, was removed as an acceptable means of settling international disputes. While the UN has not been able to resolve all forms of armed conflict, it has become a vital mechanism in the regulation and management of aggression and the use of armed force in the international system. Peace summits facilitated by the UN have come to represent a powerful symbol in the ending of wars. In entering into a peace treaty, warring factions make honourable concessions emphasizing their respect for international law enshrined in the UN Charter. Examples include the Egyptian war with Israel, which concluded with the signing of the Camp David Accords in September 1978. The UN holds firm to the belief that war is not inevitable and that differences can be managed effectively, lest they should escalate into war. However, when it comes to internal strife and civil wars, which have been on the rise since the end of the Cold War, international organizations have proven unable to resolve all forms of armed conflict.

EXTRACT FROM THE PEACE TREATY BETWEEN EGYPT AND ISRAEL, 26 MARCH 1979

Convinced of the urgent necessity of the establishment of a just, comprehensive and lasting peace in the Middle East in accordance with Security Council Resolutions 2422 and 338;

Reaffirming their adherence to the 'Framework for Peace in the Middle East Agreed at Camp David' dated September 17, 1978;

Noting that the aforementioned Framework as appropriate is intended to constitute a basis for peace not only between Egypt and Israel but also between Israel and each of its other Arab neighbors which is prepared to negotiate peace with it on this basis;

Desiring to bring to an end the state of war between them and to establish a peace in which every state in the area can live in security;

Convinced that the conclusion of a Treaty of Peace between Egypt and Israel is an important step in the search for comprehensive peace in the area and for the attainment of the settlement of the Arab-Israeli conflict in all its aspects;

Inviting the other Arab parties to this dispute to join the peace process with Israel guided by and based on the principles of the aforementioned Framework;

Desiring as well to develop friendly relations and cooperation between themselves in accordance with the United Nations Charter and the principles of international law governing international relations in times of peace;

Agree to the following provisions in the free exercise of their sovereignty, in order to implement the 'Framework for the Conclusion of a Peace Treaty Between Egypt and Israel'.

ARTICLE I

1. The state of war between the Parties will be terminated and peace will be established between them upon the exchange of instruments of ratification of this Treaty.
2. Israel will withdraw all its armed forces and civilians from the Sinai behind the international boundary between Egypt and mandated Palestine, as provided in the annexed protocol (Annex I), and Egypt will resume the exercise of its full sovereignty over the Sinai.
3. Upon completion of the interim withdrawal provided for in Annex I, the Parties will establish normal and friendly relations, in accordance with article III (3).

...

ARTICLE III

1. The Parties will apply between them the provisions of the Charter of the United Nations and the principles of international law governing relations among states in times of peace. In particular:
   a. They recognize and will respect each other's sovereignty, territorial integrity and political independence;
   b. They recognize and will respect each other's right to live in peace within their secure and recognized boundaries;
   c. They will refrain from the threat or use of force, directly or indirectly, against each other and will settle all disputes between them by peaceful means.
2. Each Party undertakes to ensure that acts or threats of belligerency, hostility, or violence do not originate from and are not committed from within its territory, or by any forces subject to its control or by any other forces stationed on its territory, against the population, citizens or property of the other Party. Each Party also undertakes to refrain from organizing, instigating, inciting, assisting or participating in acts or threats of belligerency, hostility, subversion or violence against the other Party, anywhere, and undertakes to ensure that perpetrators of such acts are brought to justice.[181]

If we accept that war is 'the continuation of political intercourse with other means', then peace must also be the continuation of that political impulse too. When it proves impossible to reconcile differences through peaceful political channels, parties in conflict might well resort to war to secure what they believe to be in their interests. To be sure, the Versailles Treaty concluded in June 1919 was designed to settle the reparations for those countries affected by the First World War and, importantly, to provide France with a guarantee of security. Unintentionally, perhaps, it had the obverse effect of feeding the right-wing desire to rearm and to restore Germany's reputation on the world stage. The peace concluded at the end of the First World War left unresolved many of the issues which caused the war in the first place. In circumstances like these a large number of disaffected Germans came to believe that their interests could only be served by resorting to war.

Victory and defeat

'Victory is the main object in war,' wrote the Chinese master of war, Sun Tzu. 'If this is long delayed, weapons are blunted and morale depressed.'[182] The Duke of Wellington's defeat of Napoleon Bonaparte at the Battle of Waterloo (1815) is regarded as one of the greatest victories in the history of warfare. In reality much of the fighting was a close-run thing. Because Napoleon did not possess outright numerical superiority at the time, argue some historians, he 'ought to have declined battle at Waterloo in the first place'.[183] The Napoleonic Wars are thought to have cost the lives of over one million soldiers and some five million civilians. The Treaties of Paris and Vienna settled territorial disputes that had arisen out of the turmoil of the 1790s and led to a long peace in European politics that would remain relatively uninterrupted by major wars until the outbreak of the First World War in 1914. This shattered peace would lead to attempts to ensure that war no longer became a legitimate means of resolving differences in foreign policy.

It was this resolve that brought into being the League of Nations in 1920, which was the forerunner of the UN. The League of Nations was formed at the close of the First World War with the intention of making it less acceptable for states to go to war with one another. It failed to check Japanese aggression in Manchuria and German aggression in Czechoslovakia. The architects of the UN came together towards the end of the Second World War with these limitations in mind and tried to reflect this in the UN Charter of 1945. But despite these inter-governmental bodies, armies are still being sent to far-off places to implement the political will of politicians in capital cities. They are also being asked in the twenty-first century to deliver victory. So is it plausible that victory in battle can still end wars? Are the vanquished prepared to stay defeated? If we look at the fighting in Syria we can see that this is the view of the security forces of dictator Bashar al-Assad and his arch-enemies in the Free Syrian Army, al-Qaeda-aligned al-Nusrah Front and Daesh. To sketch this out further we must return to the question of what these groups want and why they feel fighting will bring them closer to accomplishing their goals.

Like Tunisia, Egypt, Libya, Yemen and Bahrain, Syria was deeply affected by protests that began in 2011, centring on political corruption, nepotism, unemployment, infringement of human rights and an assortment of other grievances shared by Arabs across the Middle East and North Africa. Protests soon turned violent, and in Syria, Tunisia, Egypt and Libya, the governments' heavy-handed responses soon spiralled out of control. In Syria and Libya an upsurge of violence triggered civil wars. Within a few months Colonel Gaddafi was removed from power and killed in his home town by rebel forces. In Syria, President Assad and his troops remained embattled but militarily prepared to meet an armed challenge from their opponents. Since then much of the fighting has been bloody and intense, and has led to the deaths of over 470,000 people.[184]

For Assad, the war has been extremely damaging to his regime's control over Syrian territory. The brute force administered to civilians who opposed him showed he had no compunction when it came to ruling with an iron fist, as his father had done since the 1970s. The United States under Barack Obama threatened intervention in 2013 if Assad deployed any of his nuclear, biological or chemical weapons to maintain his tenuous grip on power. That 'red line' was crossed when the regime reportedly fired sarin gas missiles on two suburbs of Damascus. After the UK parliament rejected calls for greater intervention, Obama backed away from his initial threat, thus leaving himself at a strategic disadvantage. By 2015 President Putin of Russia had committed troops to Syria in support of the regime, as did the Iranians. Even the Shi'ite armed group Hezbollah sent fighters. In the absence of peace talks or even a vague prospect of victory, some commentators have said that the warring factions will have to exhaust themselves for there to be any significant shift in the situation.

As the Syrian case demonstrates, in seeking outright victory states are not beyond employing brute force. This does not only apply to authoritarian states either. In the irregular war fought between Britain and the Boers at the turn of the twentieth century in what is now South Africa, the British conducted a deeply attritional campaign that ended in the Treaty of Vereeniging on 31 May 1902, a peace only secured because the British realized they could no longer sustain the high price demanded in blood and treasure. A century later, Britain was facing off against another irregular opponent, this time in the form of the Taliban in Helmand Province, Afghanistan, where victory was proving just as elusive. By 2017 the armed conflict in Afghanistan looked exactly as it had a decade earlier, with regular troops locked in a stalemate with a cunning and sophisticated insurgency.

Stalemate

Stalemates are recognized as the worst possible outcome of wars, especially since they are likely to produce more grievances in the future. An obvious example of this is Sudan, which has been troubled by rebellion in the south for over a century. From the 1950s the government in Khartoum spent a considerable proportion of its budget (as much as twenty-five percent) on security to deal with warring factions. With only five percent of the budget going to development, successive governments failed to balance the books, and the consequent unrest left them susceptible to military coups.[185] The Anya-Nya separatist rebel army, active from 1969 to 1972, grew out of the lack of social and economic development in the south, the vast geographical size of the country, which made it ideal terrain for guerrillas, and the meddling of neighbouring countries in Sudan's internal affairs. As subsequent Sudanese conflicts were to prove, civil wars are frequently fought on the basis of a plethora of grievances that range from lack of socio-economic opportunity, discrimination and exclusion, to a feeling held by one or both belligerents of unfinished business.

Sudan has not been alone in seeking to end conflicts by becoming involved in a peace process. Negotiations to end fighting have been attempted elsewhere too. The struggles between the Spanish government and Basque separatist group ETA, the Colombian government and left-wing group FARC, and the Sri Lankan government and Tamil Tigers all demonstrate that conflicts do sometimes stop or pause thanks to political initiatives and expert diplomacy. Sadly, in each of these cases, the peace agreements saw belligerents enter into a process that very quickly broke down. The net result was that the states in question resorted to more vigorous action against their opponents. Only in the Colombian case has there now been a peace agreement between the two parties to the conflict, though it remains to be seen whether this will hold over the long term, especially given the presence of criminal elements who are against the deal.

Interventions

In a controversial article published in *Foreign Affairs* around the time of NATO's intervention in Kosovo in 1999, the American strategist Edward Luttwak put forward the argument that intervention by external powers in civil wars can sometimes prolong armed conflict. He felt that the displacement of peoples into refugee camps risked perpetuating the conflict long into the future. Luttwak believed that interventions undertaken by external powers for 'essentially disinterested and indeed frivolous motives' were dangerous. He argued that states ought to resist the temptation to intervene and instead allow wars to run their course 'until a resolution is reached'.[186] By doing so, he maintained, war could secure its ultimate purpose of peace.

Interventions by outside powers in wars between states and oppositional armed groups and peoples are nothing new. For centuries states have justified intervention for a variety of reasons, including national interests, humanitarian reasons, and even to prevent the overspill of conflicts into neighbouring territories or regions. During the Cold War, the number of UN-sanctioned interventions was comparatively low. After the collapse of the Soviet Union, the UN moved from paralysis of action to humanitarian interventions aimed at preventing genocide, ethnic cleansing and invasions in many countries around the world. Of course it would be wrong to claim that the UN only intervenes because of the lack of a decisive outcome in military conflict. In some cases, as we have seen, organized violence is prolonged by the absence of legitimate state authorities, which permits armed groups to proliferate (for example, in Syria, Libya and Yemen). Conflicts are also exacerbated when identity politics forms a central component of the character of war, as in cases of ethnic cleansing, genocide of minority groups, and war rape, which has been prevalent in the DRC and, more recently, in Syria. This presents its own conundrum, as liberal scholar Michael Ignatieff has observed, which 'means, of course, accepting that war may be an unavoidable solution to ethnic conflict. It means accepting a moral pact with the devil of war, seeking to use its flames to burn a path to peace.'[187]

One of the oldest examples of international intervention not resolving ethno-national conflict is Cyprus. Once an Ottoman colony, Cyprus was then gifted to the British in 1878 and continues to be of strategic importance to Britain, even after the island's declaration of independence in 1960. What is often missed in the rush to explain the nature of the international intervention after the outbreak of serious inter-communal conflict between Greek and Turkish Cypriots in December 1963 is the mounting tensions and provocations between British forces and Greek Cypriot guerrillas between 1955 and 1960, in which several hundred people were killed. A negotiated settlement eventually ended that conflict, though the reality is that after five years of irregular warfare waged in the streets, hamlets and mountains of the island, the British still retained their Sovereign Base Areas. Moreover, the conflict did not resolve the differences that arose between the Greek and Turkish Cypriot communities. In fact, many of these differences were being inflamed by nationalist groups in mainland Greece and Turkey, both of whom were named as interested parties in Cyprus's declaration of independence. This would have severe repercussions, and after Greece sent in thousands of troops and Turkey launched air strikes against the island, the UN was forced to intervene in 1964 to establish a peacekeeping force – a mission that continues over half a century later.

What made the prospect of a peaceful resolution of the Cyprus conflict even more elusive was the intervention by a

Turkish military 'peacekeeping' mission in the summer of 1974 as a response to the coup by a Greek military junta to oust Archbishop Makarios III. Until 14 August 1974, wrote journalist Christopher Hitchens, 'Cyprus had known every kind of medieval war, including siege and investment and crusade. It had also experienced conquest, colonization and exploitation. In living memory it had undergone guerrilla war, subversion and near civil war. It was now to see twentieth-century war – the real thing.'[188] In a huge military operation supported by the US, Turkey dispatched a division (numbering over 10,000 troops), which captured the ports of Famagusta, Karavostasi and Kyrenia, forcibly displacing some 250,000 Cypriots, and effectively partitioned the island. Importantly, even though the territory seized by the Turks represented only one-third of the island, it actually represented some two-thirds of the share of the Cypriot tourist industry (including the strategically important resort of Varosha in the east), a sizeable proportion of natural resources and industrial heartlands. It also divided the Cypriot capital Nicosia. Ever since, two NATO allied armies have faced one another across a no man's land known as the 'green line'.

As the UN has learnt from bitter experience, those contemplating interventions must be aware of the likelihood of being drawn in by one side or another. The UN has generally shown a reluctance to authorize Chapter VII missions where it may involve fighting wars or even a long-term occupation of a state. This is a direct result of its Charter's explicit guidelines respecting the sovereignty and territorial independence of UN member states. Nevertheless, where interventions are unavoidable, the missions most frequently authorized by the Security Council have been peacekeeping activities under Chapter VI of the UN Charter, which stresses the pacific settlement of disputes. Since the end of the Cold War, the UN has seen an exponential rise in the number of peace support operations across the world. A complementary series of actions grouped under the heading of post-conflict peace-building (where the use of force is generally minimized or not present) has also seen the UN's humanitarian-based agencies overtake the military-based, blue helmet missions in terms of their presence in conflict zones.

CHAPTER VII OF THE UN CHARTER

According to the authority vested in it by its founding Charter, the United Nations can authorize military action under two criteria. The first is self-defence. When a state is attacked it may use any means that may be necessary to defend itself. For this to be considered lawful and legitimate, the attack must be 'armed' and it must also be imminent. In the second instance armed force may be used when it is approved by the UN Security Council. Made up of five Permanent Members and ten Non-Permanent Members, the Security Council requires nine affirmative votes out of fifteen (Permanent Members can agree or abstain, but not wield their Veto) for this authorization to be passed. Examples of the Security Council authorizing the use of force include the Korean War of 1950–53, in the wake of the 9/11 attacks on the United States, and in authorizing the NATO intervention in Libya in 2011. Authorization is by no means guaranteed and Permanent Members, like the US, UK and Russia, have gone to war – in Kosovo (1999) and Iraq (2003) – without the necessary resolution authorizing the use of force. This is a risky strategy and can often bring with it much damage to international standing, to say nothing of the moral and legal questions it raises.

Building peace

Writing in the early 1990s, Marxist historian Eric Hobsbawm believed that the end of the Cold War would not necessarily end war altogether. The Falklands War, the Iran–Iraq War, and a resurgence of ethnic conflict in Europe, Asia and Africa at the time were proof to Hobsbawm that organized violence would continue well into the twenty-first century. The UN had shown itself to be powerless to prevent conflicts completely, especially during the Cold War. Nonetheless, by the early 1990s, Washington, London, Paris, Moscow and Beijing were at least more sympathetic to the prospect of collectively authorizing peace enforcement operations (under Chapter VII of the UN Charter). But after Western intervention in Kosovo (1999), Iraq (2003) and Libya (2011), the diverging national interests of the Permanent Members of the UN Security Council meant such operations would become increasingly rare.

The international community's failure to end wars by lawful, legitimate and multilateral intervention highlights one thing, namely that consensus is required for the long-term sustainability of peace-building projects. As political scientist Professor Kenneth N. Waltz would famously remark in his seminal book *Man, the State, and War*, the 'peace strategy of any one country must depend on the peace or war strategies of all other countries'. There was now widespread recognition that the UN needed to adapt to the changing realities of post-Cold War conflict. In a report he issued in 1992, the then secretary general, Boutros, Boutros-Ghali, categorized the organization's peace support activities:

> In surveying the range of efforts for peace, the concept of peace-building as the construction of a new environment should be viewed as the counterpart of preventive diplomacy, which seeks to avoid the breakdown of peaceful conditions. When conflict breaks out, mutually reinforcing efforts at peacemaking and peace-keeping come into play. Once these have achieved their objectives, only sustained, cooperative work to deal with underlying economic, social, cultural and humanitarian problems can place an achieved peace on a durable foundation. Preventive diplomacy is to avoid a crisis; post-conflict peace-building is to prevent a recurrence.[189]

Building on Boutros-Ghali's *An Agenda for Peace*, Professor Charles-Philippe David defined peace-building as:

> a concerted effort involving the parties to a conflict in a given country, the UN, and representatives of the international community to develop lasting political, economic and social infrastructures in that country. Such coordination is conducive to reconciliation and reconstruction, while also creating the conditions to prevent the resumption of armed conflict as a means of settling disputes.[190]

At the time *An Agenda for Peace* was published, post-conflict peace-building was seen as a logical progression from the breakdown of relations between parties, which resulted in crises and conflict, and the move towards a resolution of the differences that gave rise to war in the first place. Importantly, peace-building has since become increasingly responsive to the complexity of conflict and tends to focus more on the longer-term reconciliation of the parties to a conflict and the reconstruction of those societies ravaged by war. As a result, peace-building has become more global in scope, ranging from conflict resolution activities in Guatemala in Central America and Northern Ireland in western Europe, to the delivery of humanitarian aid to civil wars in Sudan in Sub-Saharan Africa and Syria in the Middle East.

Today, peace-building activities are just as likely to be initiated during conflict as they are in its aftermath, even though the UN still prefers to see peace as something that happens after a war has come to an end. As Secretary General Ban Ki-moon wrote in a report that was redolent of the conclusions drawn by one of his predecessors in the early 1990s: 'The immediate post-conflict period offers a window of opportunity to provide basic security, deliver peace dividends, shore up and build confidence in the political process, and strengthen core national capacity to lead peace-building efforts. If countries succeed in these core areas

CONFLICT RESOLUTION

The concept of conflict resolution has been around for at least half a century. It is underpinned by the view that an end to fighting may not actually bring about the termination of war unless the causes of that war are properly addressed. For conflict resolution experts, mediation between the different sides in war must result in a comprehensive peace treaty that they are all prepared to accept and work hard to sustain over the longer term. As conflict resolution relies on ensuring as inclusive a process as possible, it is generally believed that peace accords should be 'win–win' (where the parties to the conflict can claim victory, or at least, avoid defeat) rather than 'win–lose' (in which one or more parties to the conflict feel they have been defeated). As we have seen with peace treaties, from Versailles at the end of the First World War to Yemen's National Dialogue Conference almost a century later in 2014, the prospects of peace are unlikely to last if the terms of that peace treaty are considered unacceptable by one of the parties to the agreement. Even supposedly successful conflict resolution processes, like the Northern Ireland 'peace process', have not proven completely acceptable to all sides. Northern Ireland was the site of one of the world's longest-running ethnic conflicts from the late 1960s until the signing of the Good Friday Agreement in 1998. Almost twenty years on, segregation between rival groupings remains rife, terrorist groups are still very much in existence and have not moved towards demobilization, and politicians cannot agree on major policy issues. This has led prominent American mediator Richard Haass to suggest that, left unchecked, violence could re-emerge from the morass. Objectively, this has indeed been the experience of other conflicts around the world that have failed to reach acceptable peace agreements.

early on, it substantially increases the chances for sustainable peace – and reduces the risk of relapse into conflict.'[191]

The refusal of the UN to adopt a more sophisticated reading of war is interesting, especially since turning swords into ploughshares has become an even more difficult process in the twenty-first century. Peace-building experts outside national governments and international organizations like the UN have revisited the concepts of war and peace. Some, like Professor John Paul Lederach, prefer to use the language of conflict transformation (rather than resolution) in a bid to emphasize that the building of trust after war is essential if peace agreements are to be sustained. As Lederach concluded in his influential book *Building Peace* (1997):

> Most wars are located in settings on the margins of the world community that are struggling with poverty, inequalities, and underdevelopment. The lines of conflict in these settings are typically drawn along group identity lines, with the fighting aimed at achieving collective rights, in opposition to other groups of differing ethnicity, religion or race. These are long-standing conflicts. The constancy and continuance of intermediate and war levels of armed conflict defy any quick solutions or facile processes for peace.[192]

What this suggests is that we must be prepared to think about war *and* peace in a radically different way. The British general Sir Rupert Smith has given us a more convincing lens through which we might understand the dynamic interaction between war and peace:

> In the paradigm of industrial war the premise is of the sequence peace–crisis–war–resolution, which will result in peace again, with war, the military action, being the deciding factor. In the new paradigm there is no predefined sequence, but rather a continuous criss-crossing between confrontation and conflict, whilst peace is not necessarily either the starting or the end point; and whereas conflicts are ultimately resolved, this is not necessarily the case with confrontations.[193]

Our understanding of how wars end must begin from the proposition that they have not arisen because of any one single problem, nor are they likely to end according to one single solution. For we live in a world that is complex and contradictory, and where humans have not yet developed the tools or the understanding to resolve all their disputes using peaceful means.

Conclusion

Gassed, a large painting by the American artist John Singer Sargent, hangs in the Imperial War Museum, London, alongside others by Paul Nash, Stanley Spencer and Percy Wyndham Lewis. Painted by Sargent in 1919, *Gassed* has come to symbolize the death, destruction and futility of war. Men are led, hands on shoulders, many wearing blindfolds to protect their weeping and inflamed eyes, towards a medical reception station on the Western Front. Other soldiers, rendered *hors de combat* (out of action), litter the foreground of the painting. Some appear to be snatching sleep, drinking water and resting; others are clearly in shock from what they have seen and done in battle. Bodies – it is unclear whether they are alive or dead – are seen in the background, greeting another party of gassed soldiers as they are chaperoned off the battlefield, presumably towards shelter away from the fighting. Out of the smoky ruins of the mud-encased soil of the First World War, artists and poets emerged to bring us a vision of war that was both incredibly visceral and all too human in its causes, courses and consequences. It was, in many ways, representative of a dismal vision of the horrors of war, which seems to be, on the surface at least, devoid of purpose.

As one of the most intensely human of activities, there can be little doubt that war leaves a mark on the men and women who fight in it. Whether it is in an exchange of gunfire, the explosion of bombs in crowded marketplaces, or kamikaze-style suicide attacks on ships or residential housing complexes, war touches everyone caught up in its powerful gravitational pull.

To grasp the essence of war, as well as the processes that drive people to become involved in it, we must accept that war has been an accompaniment of human civilization since the earliest cave dwellers picked up axes and brandished them at others in anger. War, and the consequences of war, present mankind with a paradox. While making some people safer by engaging in it, war also, at the same time, makes others less safe. In moving from the violence of the Stone Age to the relative peace and prosperity of today's world, we are confronted by the tragic reality that we have not yet found a 'cure' for this terrible malady that has affected world history since the birth of civilization. As we discovered in previous chapters, much for this history of human evolution has also been a story of perfecting better tools for our own destruction.

Despite this, there are nonetheless those who remain cautiously optimistic about the future. Harvard professor Steven Pinker, for one, argues that violence is declining, though he also admits in his influential book *The Better Angels of Our Nature* (2011) that the future is not quite certain. At the time he wrote his book, there were grounds for optimism, with the withdrawal of Western troops from Iraq and the winding down of the NATO-led mission in Afghanistan. Pinker's thesis was also supported by notable experts on ancient warfare, like Ian Morris, who argued in 2012 that violence had dramatically decreased. However, since this research was published, dramatic fluctuations have taken place in the number of battle-related fatalities, with a rise from 87,000 deaths in 2011 to around 180,000 in 2015. Statistically, Pinker's declinist argument is nonetheless rooted in the most promising anthropological and scientific discoveries of the past few thousand years. As stated in the first chapter, we know from Morris's advanced research that at current rates only 0.7 percent of people alive today will die violently, contrasted with 1–2 percent of those in the twentieth century, 2–5 percent in ancient empires, 5–10 percent in Eurasia in the age of Steppe migrations and a startling 10–20 percent in the Stone Age. Although this might well be the case, the projected rise in the world's population, climate change, the inevitable competition over natural resources and the onset of vicious identity conflicts will most likely ensure that the numbers of wars remain constant, rather than decline further, or, for that matter, rise. Previous chapters in this book noted, for instance, how the numbers killed in internal civil wars have remained constant since 2000, principally because some ninety percent of these wars are actually reoccurrences of earlier conflicts which lacked decisive outcomes.

It should also be acknowledged that in the places where civil wars are most acute, principally the Middle East and North Africa, people do not have the luxury of picking and choosing when they should fight in wars. They do not ask, as some Westerners do, is this a 'war of choice' or a 'war of necessity'? They simply fight if that is what the situation demands of them, or they become victims of the circumstances they find themselves caught up in. In a world where states have increasingly lost their monopoly over the legitimate use of armed force, terrorist and insurgent groups have emerged to set the terms of battle. They have even become agents of mass atrocity, as we have seen with Daesh in Iraq and Syria, capitalizing on the failure of states to protect their civilian populations. These non-state actors also prey on the paralysis of the international community to come to an agreed strategy for dealing with the challenges they pose, particularly since they often use hybrid warfare to undermine their opponents.

As we have discovered throughout this book, the cost of war is enormous. When juxtaposed alongside the numbers of dead and injured, the actual expenditure by states on the running of wars is inordinately high. World military expenditure totalled almost $1.7 trillion in 2015, an increase of one percent in real terms from 2014, according to the Stockholm International Peace Research Institute (SIPRI).[194] Even though most states spend less than ten percent of their GDP on defence, this does not take into account attendant costs, such as the lives of soldiers and civilians lost or affected by war, the cost of rebuilding areas devastated by

The Percentage Share of World Military Expenditure in 2015

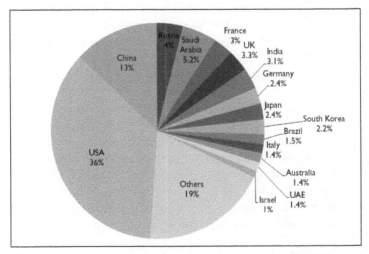

Source: Stockholm International Peace Research Institute (SIPRI)
www.sipri.org

conflict, the intellectual investment in developing weaponry and combat strategies, or, indeed, the far-reaching impact of war on the fabric of societies.

So, how long will war be with us as we move into the future? Can there ever be a world in which war is no longer mankind's method of choice when it comes to conflict resolution? If we are to follow Pinker's cautious optimism, then the answer we might put forward is: it depends. It depends on whether the UN system can adequately resolve disputes before they escalate into confrontations or armed conflict. It also depends on whether those fighting can find an alternative way of achieving their objectives more peacefully. It might even depend on whether technology can offer a less lethal (for human beings at any rate) means of achieving political objectives. In the end, though, it depends, above all, on whether enough trust can be engendered between former enemies, having suffered unimaginable horrors and loss, to resolve never again to shed blood in a bid to settle their differences.

In his 1933 novel, *The Shape of Things to Come*, H. G. Wells tells the story of a protagonist, Philip Raven, who dies and leaves behind a notebook recording his premonition of the future up to 2105. In an incredibly prescient passage, he writes:

> Everywhere in 2059 the scenery of the earth still testified to the prolonged war, the state of siege to establish a unified mastery, that had now come to an end. If most of the divisions and barriers of the period of the sovereign states had disappeared, if there were no longer castles, fortifications, boundaries and strategic lines to be traced, there were still many indications that the world was under control and still not quite sure of its own behavior.

Even though it is impossible to predict what forms war will take in the future, one thing is certain: war will remain an institution that we must confront and understand if we are ever to see an end to it.

Further reading

Introduction

For a succinct guide to the challenges posed by modern war see Richard English, *War: A Very Short Introduction* (Oxford: Oxford University Press, 2013). On ethnic conflict, see Michael Ignatieff, *The Warrior's Honor: Ethnic War and the Modern Conscience* (London: Vintage, 1999). For an analysis of the infringement of 'civilian immunity' in war, see Hugo Slim, *Killing Civilians: Method, Madness and Morality in War* (London: Hurst, 2007).

1. What is war?

On the origins and evolution of war, see John Keegan, *A History of Warfare* (London: Pimlico, 1993) and Rupert Smith, *The Utility of Force: The Art of War in the Modern World* (London: Penguin, 2005). The most comprehensive edition of Carl von Clausewitz's magisterial tome *On War* is the one edited and translated by Michael Howard and Peter Paret (Princeton, NJ: Princeton University Press, 1976). Excellent introductions to Clausewitz include Michael Howard, *Clausewitz: A Very Short Introduction* (Oxford: Oxford University Press, 2002); Beatrice Heuser, *Reading Clausewitz* (London: Pimlico, 2002); and Hew Strachan, *On War: A Biography* (London: Atlantic Books, 2007). On killing in war, see Joanna Bourke, *An Intimate History of Killing: Face to Face Killing in Twentieth Century Warfare* (London: Granta, 1999). For more detailed exposition of the morality and ethics of killing in war, see Michael Burleigh, *Moral Combat: A History of World War II*

(London: Harper Press, 2010) and Mark J. Osiel, *Making Sense of Mass Atrocity* (Cambridge: Cambridge University Press, 2009). For a historical-based, statistical analysis of the cost of war in the twentieth century, see Niall Ferguson, *The War of the World: History's Age of Hatred* (London: Allen Lane, 2006).

2. Strategy and tactics

For classic studies of strategy, see Thucydides, *History of the Peloponnesian War* (London: Penguin Books, 1972) and Sun Tzu, *The Art of War*, translated and with an introduction by Samuel B. Griffith (London: Oxford University Press, 1963). Key texts in strategic studies include J. C. Wylie, *Military Strategy: A General Theory of Power Control* (Annapolis: Naval Institute Press, 2014); Basil Liddell Hart, *Strategy: The Indirect Approach* (London: Faber, 1967); and Colin S. Gray, *Modern Strategy* (Oxford: Oxford University Press, 1999). On the history of tactics in war, see Paddy Griffith, *Forward into Battle: Fighting Tactics from Waterloo to the Near Future – Revised and Updated Edition* (Ramsbury: Crowood Press, 1990).

3. Regular war

The orthodox understanding of so-called 'old wars' has been challenged by Mary Kaldor, *New and Old Wars: Organized Violence in a Global Era – Second Edition* (Cambridge: Polity, 2006). For a classic text on war at sea, see Admiral Sir H. W. Richmond, *Naval Warfare* (London: Ernest Benn Limited, 1930). War in the air is covered by Giulio Douhet, *The Command of the Air* (London: Faber and Faber, 1943). We are well served with excellent studies of the First World War, such as Niall Ferguson, *The Pity of War* (London: Allen Lane, 1998); Hew Strachan, *The First World War, Volume 1: To Arms* (Oxford: Oxford University Press, 2001); and Gary Sheffield, *A Short History of the First World War* (London: Oneworld, 2014). On the Second World War, see H. P. Willmott, *The Great Crusade: A New Complete History of the Second World War – Revised Edition* (Dulles, VA: Potomac Books, 2008) and, more recently, Antony Beevor, *The Second World War* (London: Weidenfeld & Nicolson, 2012).

4. Irregular war

On Roman warfare, see the classic text by Caesar, *The Conquest of Gaul* (London: Penguin, 1951) and, more recently, by Peter S. Wells, *The Battle That Stopped Rome: Emperor Augustus, Arminius, and the Slaughter of the Legions in the Teutoburg Forest* (New York: W. W. Norton, 2003). For a classic text on irregular war, see Mao Tse-Tung, *Selected Military Writings of Mao Tse-Tung* (Peking: Foreign Languages Press, 1963). A scholarly analysis of post-Maoist revolutionary warfare can be found in John Mackinlay, *The Insurgent Archipelago: from Mao to bin Laden* (London: Hurst & Company, 2009). On the Soviet war in Afghanistan, see Rodric Braithwaite, *Afghantsy: The Russians in Afghanistan, 1979–89* (London, Profile Books, 2011). Important critiques of Western approaches to counter-insurgency in the early twenty-first century can be found in Frank Ledwidge, *Losing Small Wars: British Military Failure in Iraq and Afghanistan* (London: Yale, 2011) and Colonel Gian Gentile, *Wrong Turn: America's Deadly Embrace of Counterinsurgency* (New York: The New Press, 2013). One of the best analyses of insurgency in South-West Asia is Ahmed Rashid, *Taliban: The Power of Militant Islam in Afghanistan and Beyond* (London: I.B. Tauris, [2000] 2010), while readers are well served by Jason Burke's thorough treatment of Islamist terrorism, *Al-Qaeda: The True Story of Radical Islam – Updated Edition* (London: Penguin Books, 2007).

5. Future war

For three of the most important contributions to the debate on the likely direction of future war, see Martin Van Creveld, *The Transformation of War* (New York: Free Press, 1991); Colin S. Gray, *Another Bloody Century: Future Warfare* (London: Weidenfeld & Nicolson, 2005); and Christopher Coker, *Future War* (Cambridge: Polity, 2015). On technology and warfare, see Michael White, *The*

Fruits of War: How Military Conflict Accelerates Technology (London: Pocket Books, 2005) and P. W. Singer, *Wired for War: The Robotics Revolution and Conflict in the 21st Century* (London: Penguin, 2009).

6. Ending wars

One of the most influential books on peace-building is John Paul Lederach, *Building Peace: Sustainable Reconciliation in Divided Societies* (Washington, DC: United States Institute of Peace Press, 1997). For a succinct and influential critique of the peace studies tradition, see Michael Howard, *The Invention of Peace: Reflections on War and International Order* (London: Yale University Press, 2001).

7. Leaders and followers

The classic study of command and leadership in war is John Keegan, *The Mask of Command* (London: Jonathan Cape, 1987). However, there is a plethora of books on leadership and war available. One of the best from the point of view of a practitioner in the so-called '9/11 Wars' is General Stanley McChrystal, *My Share of the Task: A Memoir* (London: Portfolio, 2013). On followers in war, see another classic offering from John Keegan, *The Face of Battle: A Study of Agincourt, Waterloo and the Somme* (London: Pimlico, 1991) and the more recent and thorough meditations on the concept of 'followership' by Barbara Kellerman, *The End of Leadership* (New York: HarperCollins, 2012).

Conclusion

For more on the debate surrounding the apparent decline of violence in the modern world, see Steven Pinker, *The Better Angels of Our Nature: The Decline of Violence in History and its Causes* (London: Allen Lane, 2011) and Ian Morris, *War – What is it Good For? The Role of Conflict in Civilisation, from Primates to Robots* (London: Profile Books, 2014).

Notes

1   Statistics and maps outlining the state of war in the modern world can be found in the International Institute for Strategic Studies annual *Armed Conflict Survey*, vol. 1, no. 1 (London: IISS, 2015).

2   Richard Norton-Taylor, 'Global armed conflicts becoming more deadly, major study finds', *Guardian*, 20 May 2015. Other reports, such as the *Global Peace Index 2016*, published by the Institute for Economics and Peace, have noted how battle-related deaths have increased five-fold since 2008 and deaths as a result of terrorism have increased by 286 percent. See Institute for Economics and Peace, *Global Peace Index 2016* (New York: Institute for Economics and Peace, 2016), p. 24. Archived at: reliefweb.int/sites/reliefweb.int/files/resources/GPI%202016%20Report_2.pdf (accessed 2 July 2016).

3   Statistics on Iraq and Syria are taken from www.Iraqibodycount.org and Syrian Centre for Policy Research (SCPR), http://scpr-syria.org.

4   Institute for Economics and Peace, *Global Peace Index 2015* (New York: Institute for Economics and Peace, 2015), p. 45. Archived at: http://economicsandpeace.org/wp-content/uploads/2015/06/Global-Peace-Index-Report-2015_0.pdf (accessed 2 July 2016).

5   Carl von Clausewitz, *On War*, edited and translated by Michael Howard and Peter Paret (Princeton, NJ: Princeton University Press, 1976), p. 89.

6   George Orwell, 'Can socialists be happy?', *Tribune*, 20 December 1943, http://theorwellprize.co.uk/george-orwell/by-orwell/essays-and-other-works/can-socialists-be-happy/ (accessed 9 May 2016).

7   Cyril Falls, *Ordeal by Battle* (London: Methuen, 1943), p. 9.

8   Steven Pinker, *The Better Angels of Our Nature: The Decline of Violence in History and its Causes* (London: Allen Lane, 2011), p. 39.

9   Ian Morris, *War – What is it Good For? The Role of Conflict in Civilisation, from Primates to Robots* (London: Profile Books, 2014), p. 333.

10   Sun Tzu, *The Art of War*, translated and with an introduction by Samuel B. Griffith (London: Oxford University Press, 1963), pp. 63, 73.

11   Niall Ferguson, *The Pity of War* (London: Allen Lane, 1998), p. 346.

12   John Keegan, *The Face of Battle: A Study of Agincourt, Waterloo and the Somme* (London: Pimlico, 1991), p. 324.

13   Thucydides, *History of the Peloponnesian War* (London: Penguin, [1954] 1972), pp. 158–9.

14   Mark J. Osiel, *Obeying Orders: Atrocity, Military Discipline and the Law of War* (New Brunswick, NJ: Transaction Publishers, 1999), p. 7.

15   Ian Gardiner, *The Yompers: With 45 Commando in the Falklands War* (Barnsley: Pen and Sword, 2012), p. 189.

16   F. T. Moneta, 'What is war?', *The Advocate of Peace, Boston*, 56:2 (February 1894), p. 29.

17   Rupert Brooke, *1914 and Other Poems* (London: Sidgwick and Jackson, 1916), p. 11.

18   S. L. A. Marshall, *Men Against Fire* (Gloucester, MA: Peter Smith, 1978).

19   Lieutenant Colonel Dave Grossman, *On Killing: The Psychological Cost of Learning to Kill in War and Society* (London: Little, Brown, 1995), p. 31.

20   Ernest Hemingway, *For Whom the Bell Tolls* (London: Arrow Books, [1941] 2004), p. 333.

21   Sean Hemingway, 'Introduction', in Ernest Hemingway, *Hemingway on War* (London: Vintage, 2014), p. xxi.

22   Leon Trotsky, 'Our current basic military tasks', 1 April 1922, in Leon Trotsky, *Military Writings* (New York: Pathfinder Press, 1971), p. 90.

23   J. F. C. Fuller, *War and Western Civilisation, 1832–1932: A Study of War as a Political Instrument and the Expression of Mass Democracy* (London: Duckworth, 1932), p. 225.

24   Martha Gellhorn, *The Face of War* (London: Virago Press, [1936] 1986), p. 58.

25   Correspondence with a British Army Iraq War veteran, 21 December 2014.

26   George Orwell, *Homage to Catalonia* (London: Penguin Books, [1938] 1962), p. 71.

27   Randall Collins, 'The micro-sociology of violence', *British Journal of Sociology*, 60:3 (2009), p. 568.

28   Hannah Arendt, *On Violence* (Orlando, FA: Harcourt Books, 1969), pp. 35–56.

29   Richard Holmes, *Firing Line* (London: Penguin, 1985), p. 204.

30   Ibid., p. 149.

31   The National Archives, WO 361/770, Alexander Hospital, Singapore, Events of 14/15 Feb. 1942.

32   Gore Vidal, *Dreaming War: Blood for Oil and the Cheney-Bush Junta* (New York: Thunder's Mouth Press/Nation Books, 2002), p. 103.

33   For more on this point, see the empirical research by Alexander Laban Hinton on the Khmer Rouge: 'Why did you kill? The Cambodian genocide and the dark side of face and honor', *Journal of Asian Studies*, 571 (February 1998), pp. 93–122, and also James Waller, *Becoming Evil: How Ordinary People Commit Genocide and Mass Killing* (Oxford: Oxford University Press, 2007).

34   Michael Burleigh, *Moral Combat: A History of World War II* (London: Harper Press, 2010), p. 360.

35   William Thomas Allison, *My Lai: An American Atrocity in the Vietnam War* (Baltimore: Johns Hopkins University Press, 2012), p. 40.

36   James S. Olson and Randy Roberts, *My Lai: A Brief History with Documents* (Boston: Bedford/St Martin's, 1998), p. 112.

37   Frederick Downs, *The Killing Zone: My Life in the Vietnam War* (London: W. W. Norton, [1978] 1993), p. 216.

38   Eric Hobsbawm, 'Barbarism: a user's guide', in Eric Hobsbawm, *On History* (New York: New Press, 1997), p. 257.

39   Charles Guthrie and Michael Quinlan, *Just War: The Just War Tradition: Ethics in Modern Warfare* (New York: Walker and Company, 2007), p. 46.

40   Mark J. Osiel, *Making Sense of Mass Atrocity* (Cambridge: Cambridge University Press, 2009), p. 7.

41   Lieutenant General Roméo Dallaire, *Shake Hands with the Devil: The Failure of Humanity in Rwanda* (London: Arrow Books, 2003), p. 430.

42   For more information on the problem of sexual violence in conflict and in peace, see the UN's Stop Rape Now campaign at http://www.stoprapenow.org.

43   The Baha Mousa Public Inquiry, Witness Statement of Gareth Aspinall to the Baha Mousa Public Inquiry, dated 14 October 2009,

http://webarchive.nationalarchives.gov.uk/20120215203912/
http://www.bahamousainquiry.org/linkedfiles/baha_mousa/
baha_mousa_inquiry_evidence/evidence_091109/bmi05211.pdf
(accessed 9 May 2015).

44   A. T. Williams, *A Very British Killing: The Death of Baha Mousa*
(London: Jonathan Cape, 2012), p. 291.

45   OHCHR, *Report of the United Nations Office of the High Commis-
sioner for Human Rights Investigation on Sri Lanka* (OISL) (16
September 2015), http://www.ohchr.org/EN/HRBodies/HRC/
Pages/OISL.aspx (accessed 2 July 2016).

46   Andrew Hosken, *Empire of Fear: Inside the Islamic State* (London:
Oneworld, 2015), p. 187.

47   Mao Tse-Tung, 'Problems of strategy in China's Revolutionary
War, December 1936', in Mao Tse-Tung, *Selected Military Writings
of Mao Tse-Tung* (Peking: Foreign Languages Press, 1963), p. 79.

48   Clausewitz, *On War*, p. 177.

49   Stephen Biddle, 'Strategy in war', *PS: Political Science and Politics*,
40:3 (July 2007), p. 464.

50   Colin S. Gray, *Modern Strategy* (Oxford: Oxford University Press,
1999), p. 17. Emphasis in original.

51   J. C. Wylie, *Military Strategy: A General Theory of Power Control*
(Annapolis: Naval Institute Press, [1967] 2014), p. 9.

52   Thucydides, *History of the Peloponnesian War*, p. 299.

53   Sun Tzu, *The Art of War*, p. 77.

54   Clausewitz, *On War*, p. 88.

55   Tim Bean, 'Naval warfare in the Pacific, 1941–5', in Simon Trew
and Gary Sheffield (eds), *100 Years of Conflict, 1900–2000* (Stroud:
Sutton Publishing, 2000), p. 193.

56   H. P. Willmott, *The Great Crusade: A New Complete History of the
Second World War* (London: Pimlico, 1989), p. 160.

57   Leon Trotsky, 'Marxism and military knowledge, 8 May 1922', in
Trotsky, *Military Writings*, p. 141.

58   General Stanley McChrystal, *My Share of the Task: A Memoir*
(London: Portfolio, 2013), pp. 349–50.

59   Christopher Bayly and Tim Harper, *Forgotten Armies: The Fall of
British Asia, 1941–1945* (London: Allen Lane, 2004), p. 106.

60 Julian Corbett, *Some Principles of Maritime Strategy* (London: Longmans, Green and Co., [1911] 1938), p. 78.

61 Clausewitz, *On War*, p. 128 (original emphasis).

62 Antony Beevor, *The Second World War* (London: Weidenfeld & Nicolson, 2012), p. 131.

63 Ibid., p. 133.

64 Correlli Barnett, *Britain and Her Army, 1509–1970: A Military, Political and Social Survey* (London: Allen Lane, 1970), p. 323.

65 Michael White, *The Fruits of War: How Military Conflict Accelerates Technology* (London: Pocket Books, 2005), p. 175.

66 S. P. Oakley, 'Single combat in the Roman Republic', *Classical Quarterly: New Series*, 35:2 (1985), p. 405.

67 Michael Roberts, 'The military revolution, 1560–1660', in Michael Roberts (ed.), *Essays in Swedish History* (London: Weidenfeld & Nicolson, 1967), p. 197.

68 War Office, *The Training and Employment of Platoons 1918* (London: War Office, February 1918), p. 10.

69 Gary Sheffield, *A Short History of the First World War* (London: Oneworld, 2014), p. 68.

70 Ibid.

71 J. F. C. Fuller, *War and Western Civilization, 1832–1932: A Study of War as a Political Instrument and the Expression of Mass Democracy* (London: Duckworth, 1932), p. 226.

72 Admiral Sir H. W. Richmond, *Naval Warfare* (London: Ernest Benn Limited, 1930), p. 11.

73 Clausewitz, *On War*, p. 580.

74 Ibid., p. 627.

75 Chris Bellamy, *Absolute War – Soviet Russia in the Second World War: A Modern History* (London: Macmillan, 2007), p. 2.

76 General Erich Ludendorff, *My War Memories, 1914–1918* (London: Hutchinson and Company, 1919), p. 3.

77 Ibid., p. 333.

78 Tony Judt with Timothy Snyder, *Thinking the Twentieth Century* (London: Vintage, 2012), p. 125.

79 Howard Zinn, *A People's History of the United States, 1492–Present* (New York: HarperPerennial, 2005), p. 237.

80   The Whitehouse, *The National Security Strategy of the United States of America* (Washington, DC: White House, September 2002), p. 15 (emphasis added).

81   An analysis of the battle can be found in Geoffrey Till, *Maritime Strategy and the Nuclear Age: Second Edition* (London: Macmillan, 1984), p. 92.

82   Statistics taken from official NATO figures, 'The Kosovo Air Campaign (Archived): Operation Allied Force', http://www.nato.int/cps/en/natohq/topics_49602.htm (accessed 9 May 2016).

83   George Robertson, 'War in Kosovo: some preliminary lessons', *RUSI Journal*, 144:4 (August 1999), pp. 1–6.

84   Giulio Douhet, *The Command of the Air* (London: Faber and Faber, 1943), p. 83.

85   Lawrence Freedman, *The Official History of the Falklands Campaign, Vol. II: War and Diplomacy* (London: Routledge, 2005), pp. 772–4.

86   Speech delivered by British prime minister Margaret Thatcher to the House of Commons on 14 April 1982. UK House of Commons Debates (Hansard), 14 April 1982, vol. 21, col. 1146.

87   William Philpott, *Bloody Victory: The Sacrifice on the Somme and the Making of the Twentieth Century* (London: Little, Brown, 2009), p. 95.

88   Russell A. Hart, *Clash of Arms: How the Allies Won in Normandy* (Oklahoma: University of Oklahoma Press, 2004), p. 248.

89   Max Hastings, *Overlord: D-Day and the Battle for Normandy* (London: Pan Books, 1984), p. 148.

90   Clausewitz, *On War*, p. 204.

91   Phillip Killicoat, 'Weaponomics: the global market for assault rifles', World Bank Policy Research Working Paper 4202, Post-Conflict Transitions Working Paper No. 10 (Oxford University, April 2007), p. 3.

92   Mikhail Kalashnikov with Elena Joly, *The Gun that Changed the World* (Cambridge: Polity Press, 2006), p. 95.

93   Sun Tzu, *The Art of War*, p. 102.

94   Basil Liddell Hart, *The Other Side of the Hill* (London: Macmillan, [1948] 1993), p. 126.

95   Interview with General Sir Roger Wheeler, 23 February 2011.

96   Rupert Smith, *The Utility of Force: The Art of War in the Modern World* (London: Penguin, 2005), p. 390.

97 H. E. L. Mellersh, *Soldiers of Rome* (London: Robert Hale, 1964), p. 37.

98 Frank Hoffman, *Conflict in the 21ˢᵗ Century: The Rise of Hybrid Wars* (Arlington, VA: Potomac Institute for Policy Studies, 2007), archived at: http://www.potomacinstitute.org/images/stories/publications/potomac_hybridwar_0108.pdf (accessed 26 June 2016).

99 Sam Jones, 'Ukraine: Russia's new art of war', *Financial Times*, 28 August 2014.

100 Cyril Falls, *The Art of War: From the Age of Napoleon to the Present Day* (London: Oxford University Press, 1961), p. 82.

101 Michael Collins, *The Path to Freedom* (Wales: Welsh Academic Press, [1922] 1996), p. 69.

102 Ibid., p. 69.

103 Ibid., p. 70. My emphasis.

104 Fidel Castro, *My Life* (London: Allen Lane, 2007), pp. 177–8.

105 Edgar Snow, *Red Star Over China* (London: Victor Gollancz Ltd., 1937), p. 288.

106 Joanna Wright, 'Weapon of choice: militants modify IEDs to evade counter-measures', *Jane's Intelligence Review*, 26:8 (August 2014), pp. 8–13.

107 Michael Sheehan, 'The changing character of war', in John Baylis, Steve Smith and Patricia Owens (eds), *The Globalization of World Politics: An Introduction to International Relations – Fourth Edition* (Oxford: Oxford University Press, 2008), p. 214.

108 Karan Thapar, 'Russians switch to commando-type raids in Afghanistan', *The Times*, 19 September 1980.

109 Richard Dowden, 'Troops tell of Afghan atrocities', *The Times*, 28 June 1984.

110 Rodric Braithwaite, *Afghantsy: The Russians in Afghanistan, 1979–89* (London, Profile Books, [2011] 2012), p. 272.

111 Anatol Lieven, 'Jalalabad pounded by 3,000 rebel rockets', *The Times*, 13 March 1989.

112 Carlos Marighella, *For the Liberation of Brazil*, translated by John Butt and Rosemary Sheed (London: Penguin, 1971), p. 181.

113 Australian War Memorial, 1 ATF Documents, Brief for the Minister of External Affairs – Notes on Current Enemy Situation in

MR3 (as at Oct 1970), notes used in a briefing of JIO representatives on 20 November 1970.

114 Ibid.

115 Ibid.

116 Australian Government, Department of Veterans' Affairs, 'The Vietnam War', http://vietnam-war.commemoration.gov.au/vietnam-war/index.php (accessed 9 May 2016).

117 Interview with a former commanding officer of 22 SAS, April 2013.

118 Colonel Charlie Beckwith, *Delta Force: The Army's Elite Counterterrorist Unit* (New York: Avon Books, 1983), p. 40.

119 General Wesley K. Clark, *Winning Modern Wars: Iraq, Terrorism, and the American Empire* (New York: Public Affairs, 2003), p. 95.

120 Gregory Fremont-Barnes, 'Introduction', in Gregory Fremont-Barnes (ed.), *A History of Counterinsurgency – Volume 1: From South Africa to Algeria, 1900–1954* (Santa Barbara, CA: Praeger, 2015), p. 1.

121 Colonel Gian Gentile, *Wrong Turn: America's Deadly Embrace of Counterinsurgency* (New York: New Press, 2013), p. 13.

122 Thomas Keaney and Thomas Rid, 'Understanding counterinsurgency', in Thomas Rid and Thomas Keaney (eds), *Understanding Counterinsurgency: Doctrine, Operations, and Challenges* (Abingdon: Routledge, 2010), p. 1.

123 Alexander Alderson, 'Britain', in Rid and Keaney (eds), *Understanding Counterinsurgency*, p. 40.

124 General Stanley McChrystal, 'Lesson from Iraq: it takes a network to defeat a network', *LinkedIn*, 21 June 2013.

125 James A. Russell, 'Innovation in war: counterinsurgency operations in Anbar and Ninewa Provinces, Iraq, 2005–2007', *Journal of Strategic Studies*, 33:4 (August 2010), pp. 595–624 (p. 599).

126 Barry Rubin, 'Israel's new strategy', *Foreign Affairs*, 85:4 (July–August 2006), p. 112.

127 Peter Paret, *The Cognitive Challenge of War: Prussia, 1806* (Oxford: Princeton University Press, 2009).

128 Douhet, *The Command of the Air*, p. 119.

129 Smith, *The Utility of Force*, p. 372.

130 Martin Van Creveld, *The Transformation of War* (New York: Free Press, 1991), pp. 197–8.

131 General Charles C. Krulak, Statement of Commandant of the United States Marine Corps before the Senate Armed Services Committee on 29th September 1998 Concerning Posture, http://fas.org/man/congress/1998/980929ck.htm (accessed 9 May 2016).

132 DoD, DoD News Briefing – Secretary Rumsfeld and Gen. Myers, 12 February 2002, http://archive.defense.gov/transcripts/transcript.aspx?transcriptid=2636 (accessed 2 July 2016).

133 Dylan Love, 'Steve Jobs' 13 most inspiring quotes', *Business Insider*, 13 April 2014.

134 Wylie, *Military Strategy*, p. 93.

135 Christopher Hitchens, 'So is this war?', *Guardian*, 13 September 2001.

136 George Orwell, 'Notes on nationalism', in George Orwell, *Decline of the English Murder and Other Essays* (London: Penguin, 1965), pp. 158–9.

137 David Kilcullen, *Out of the Mountains: The Coming Age of the Urban Guerrilla* (London: Hurst, 2013), p. 262.

138 Statistics taken from the Bureau of Investigative Journalism Covert Drone War Database, https://www.thebureauinvestigates.com/category/projects/drones/drones-graphs/ (accessed 9 May 2016). The figures are taken from the upper end of the casualty figures.

139 United States Senate Judiciary Committee Subcommittee on the Constitution, Civil Rights and Human Rights Drone Wars: The Constitutional and Counterterrorism Implications of Targeted Killing Statement of Farea Al-Muslimi, 23 April 2013, http://www.judiciary.senate.gov/imo/media/doc/04-23-13Al-MuslimiTestimony.pdf (accessed 22 May 2015).

140 Anna Mulrine, 'CIA chief Leon Panetta: the next Pearl Harbor could be a cyberattack', *Christian Science Monitor*, 9 June 2011, http://www.csmonitor.com/USA/Military/2011/0609/CIA-chief-Leon-Panetta-The-next-Pearl-Harbor-could-be-a-cyberattack (accessed 9 May 2016).

141 Thomas Rid, *Cyber War Will Not Take Place* (London: Hurst & Company, 2013), p. 166.

142 Tanisha M. Fazal, 'Dead wrong? Battle deaths, military medicine, and exaggerated reports of war's demise', *International Security*, 39:1 (Summer, 2014), p. 122.

143 Émile Zola, *The Debacle [1870–71]* (London: Penguin Books, 1972), pp. 122–3.

144 Eric Hobsbawm, *The Age of Revolution, 1789–1848* (New York: Vintage Books, [1962] 1996), pp. 74–5.

145 Paul Cartledge, *Alexander the Great: The Truth Behind the Myth* (London: Pan Books, [2004] 2013), p. 157.

146 George Bernard Shaw, *Everybody's Political What's What?* (London: Constable, 1944), p. 123.

147 For more on the transformation of leadership, see Barbara Kellerman, *The End of Leadership* (New York: HarperCollins, 2012).

148 Keith Grint, *Leadership: Limits and Possibilities* (Basingstoke: Palgrave, 2005), p. 39.

149 McChrystal, *My Share of the Task*, p. 391.

150 Anthony McIntyre, 'Ride on', *The Blanket*, 24 February 2008, http://indiamond6.ulib.iupui.edu:81/AMDARK2.html (accessed 9 May 2016).

151 Dolores Price, 'Brendan Hughes: comrade and friend', *The Blanket*, 17 February 2008, http://indiamond6.ulib.iupui.edu:81/DPBH08.html (accessed 9 May 2016).

152 Jorge Castaneda, *Companero: The Life and Death of Che Guevara* (London: Bloomsbury, 1997), p. 120.

153 Fidel Castro, *My Life* (London: Allen Lane, 2007), p. 193.

154 *Magazin für deutsche Geschichte und Statistik* (1784), cited in Christopher Duffy, *The Military Experience in the Age of Reason* (London: Routledge and Kegan Paul, 1987), p. 91.

155 Ibid., pp. 89–90.

156 Liddell Hart Centre for Military Archives (LHCMA), General Sir Hughie Stockwell Papers, 6/26, 'Lessons learned in Palestine', 17 November 1948.

157 Pierre Boulle, *The Bridge over the River Kwai* (London: Fontana, [1954] 1975).

158 Ibid., p. 73.

159 Zola, *The Debacle*, p. 199.

160 Cited in Richard Holmes, *Soldiers: Army Lives and Loyalties from Redcoats to Dusty Warriors* (London: Harper Press, 2011), pp. xvi–xvii.

161 Eric Hobsbawm, *The Age of Empire, 1875–1914* (New York: Vintage Books, 1987), p. 305.

162 Gore Vidal, 'Westpoint', *New York Review of Books*, 18 October 1973. Cited in Gore Vidal, *United States: Essays, 1952–1992* (London: Abacus, 1994), p. 1089.

163 Bao Ninh, *The Sorrow of War* (London: Vintage Books, [1991] 1998), p. 15.

164 Ibid., p. 17.

165 CAIN, *Text of Irish Republican Army (IRA) 'Green Book' (Book I and II)* (no date), http://cain.ulst.ac.uk/othelem/organ/ira/ira_green_book.htm (accessed 9 May 2016).

166 Anthony Lloyd, *My War Gone By, I Miss It So* (New York: Grove Press, 1999), pp. 110–11.

167 Ibid., p. 111.

168 Asne Seierstad, *The Angel of Grozny: Inside Chechnya* (London: Virago Press, 2008), p. 296.

169 Spirit of Hiroshima, 'My best appreciation to my teacher who saved my life to overcome agony and live strongly: The story of Taeko Teramae'. Archived at: http://www.hiroshima-spirit.jp/en/voice/teramae_e.html#teramae1_E (accessed 29 August 2016).

170 Harry S. Truman Library and Museum, 'Press release by the White House, 6 August 1945', Subject File, Ayers Papers, http://www.trumanlibrary.org/whistlestop/study_collections/bomb/large/documents/index.php?documentdate=1945-08-06&documentid=59&studycollectionid=abomb&pagenumber=1 (accessed 9 May 2016).

171 Ward Wilson, 'The myth of nuclear necessity', *New York Times*, 13 January 2013, http://www.nytimes.com/2013/01/14/opinion/the-myth-of-nuclear-necessity.html?ref=opinion&_r=0 (accessed 2 July 2016).

172 US National Archives and Records Administration, Japanese Instrument of Surrender, dated 2 September 1945, http://www.archives.gov/exhibits/featured_documents/japanese_surrender_document/ (accessed 9 May 2016).

173 This quotation is frequently misattributed to Plato, but the phrase can be found in George Santayana, *Soliloquies in England and Later Soliloquies* (London: Constable and Company, 1922), p. 102.

174 Basil Liddell Hart, *Strategy: The Indirect Approach* (London: Faber, 1967), p. 351.

175 Clausewitz, *On War*, p. 81.

176 P. Sahadevan, 'Ending ethnic war: the South Asian experience', *International Negotiation*, 8:2 (2003), p. 427.

177 Dan Smith, *Trends and Causes of Armed Conflict – Edited Version* (Berlin: Berghof Research Centre for Constructive Conflict Management, August 2004), p. 4.

178 World Bank, *World Development Report: Conflict, Security and Development* (Washington, DC: World Bank, 2011), p. 3.

179 Charles T. Call and Elizabeth M. Cousins, 'Ending wars and building peace: international responses to war-torn societies', *International Studies Perspectives*, 9 (2008), p. 2.

180 John M. Mathews, 'The termination of war', *Michigan Law Review*, 19:8 (June 1921), p. 819.

181 UN, Peace Treaty between Egypt and Israel, 26 March 1979, http://peacemaker.un.org/sites/peacemaker.un.org/files/EG%20IL_790326_Egypt%20and%20Israel%20Treaty%20of%20Peace.pdf (accessed 9 May 2016).

182 Sun Tzu, *The Art of War*, p. 73.

183 Gregory Fremont-Barnes, *Waterloo, 1815: The British Army's Day of Destiny* (Stroud: History Press, 2014), p. 304.

184 'Quantifying carnage: how many people has Syria's civil war killed?', *The Economist*, 20 February 2016.

185 David Roden, 'Regional inequality and rebellion in the Sudan', *Geographical Review*, 64:4 (October 1974), p. 513.

186 Edward Luttwak, 'Give war a chance', *Foreign Affairs*, 78:4 (July–August 1999), p. 36.

187 Michael Ignatieff, *The Warrior's Honor: Ethnic War and the Modern Conscience* (London: Vintage, 1999), p. 160.

188 Christopher Hitchens, *Cyprus* (London: Quartet Books, 1984), p. 100.

189 UN, *An Agenda for Peace, Preventive Diplomacy, Peacemaking and Peace-keeping* dated 17 June 1992, Report of the Secretary-General pursuant to the statement adopted by the Summit Meeting of the Security Council on 31 January 1992 (New York: UN, 1992), http://www.un.org/ga/search/view_doc.asp?symbol=A/47/277 (accessed 9 May 2016).

190 Charles-Philippe David, 'Does peacebuilding build peace? Liberal (mis)steps in the peace process', *Security Dialogue*, 30:1 (1999), p. 28.

191 UN, *Report of the Secretary-General on Peacebuilding in the Immediate Aftermath of Conflict* (New York: UN, 11 June 2009), http://www. un.org/ga/search/view_doc.asp?symbol=A/63/881 (accessed 9 May 2016), p. 3.

192 John Paul Lederach, *Building Peace: Sustainable Reconciliation in Divided Societies* (Washington, DC: United States Institute of Peace Press, 1997), p. 17.

193 Smith, *The Utility of Force*, p. 181.

194 SIPRI, 'World military spending resumes upward course, says SIPRI', 5 April 2016, http://www.sipri.org/media/pressreleases/2016/ milex-apr-2016 (accessed 9 May 2016).

Index